Annette Wolter

Parakeets

Everything about Purchase,
Care, Nutrition,
Breeding, and Behavior

Filled with Full-color Photographs

Illustrations by
Karin Heckel

BARRON'S

2 CONTENTS

CONSIDERATIONS BEFORE BUYING

Parakeets include a great variety of bird species that are widely distributed throughout Asia, South America, Africa, and Australia. The parakeet discussed in this book is most often called a "budgie." This particular species originated in Australia, where it was given the Australian aborigine name "betcherrigah," or "budgerigar," which stands for "good bird." In 1840 a few budgies were brought to England, where their popularity grew very rapidly. The birds were bred in great numbers, and most of the parakeets that you see in pet stores today are descendants of these parakeets or budgies.

Parakeets like to be included in everything. Sitting on a human shoulder, being gently scratched, and conversing with "their" humans—this is what life can be like if the owners have enough time to devote to their bird. If you don't have much time, you should buy two parakeets. Life with a parakeet is never dull, and the entertainment can last for at least 12 years; parakeets that are kept properly can live that long.

If your dream is to have a parakeet that will become a friendly member of the family and a cheerful friend, remember that this intelligent

Parakeets love to have company: if possible, it is best to keep at least two of these colorful birds.

small bird also has some desires and requirements for its life with you. It wants affection, human company, freedom to fly, branches for climbing around on, things to nibble on, toys to toss to the floor, someone to pick them up again, and so on. To make sure there won't be any problems later, here are a few points to consider:

1. A parakeet can live 12 to 14 years. Are you prepared to assume responsibility for a pet for that long?

2. Do you have a suitable place for the cage?

3. How will you react if your parakeet remains shy and timid and refuses to speak?

4. Do you have enough time to devote to a parakeet?

5. Who will play with the parakeet and whistle tunes to it? Without this kind of attention the bird will be bored.

6. What will happen to it when you go away on vacation or if you are ill and have to go to the hospital?

7. Are there other pets in the household that might not get along with the bird? A dog can be taught not to touch the bird, but cats don't respond to such training.

8. Are you planning to give the parakeet to your child as a present? If so, it will still be up to you to watch out for the bird.

9. Are you sure that no one in your family is allergic to bird feathers?

10. Remember that having a bird will cost money, especially if the services of a veterinarian are needed at some point.

Male or Female?

It doesn't matter whether you choose a male or a female, but in the case of a young bird, only an expert can tell with any certainty what sex it is. With adult parakeets the male can usually be recognized because its cere, a soft, waxlike covering on the base of the upper mandible, is blue. All females have beige to brownish ceres. In some special color varieties, however, this sure way of telling the sexes apart doesn't work because the male, too, has a beige cere. If a bird is young, healthy, and lively, its sex is of little consequence.

It is not true that only males can be tamed and can learn to speak. I know many female parakeets that chatter away amusingly and are very friendly.

It is true, however, that females have a greater need to nibble and gnaw, for in nature it is the female that works away at a hole in a tree with her bill until the entry hole and the nesting cavity are just right.

One Bird or a Pair?

Most people want only one parakeet and hope that their bird will be tame, friendly, and playful, take a lively interest in its owner's life, perhaps learn to talk, and be cheerful and happy. Few people realize or give any thought to how much time has to be spent with a bird for it to become this trusting and not to succumb to boredom and apathy. Parakeets are by nature gregarious birds. They are dependent on the community of their flock, and especially on the company of their lifelong mate. A parakeet that is kept as a pet will be happy only if it can develop a strong bond to a human who serves as a surrogate partner. For such a relationship to develop, this human partner must be around the bird frequently and must actively play with the bird, talk to it, whistle tunes to it, and be physically affectionate toward it. Anyone who is often away from home because of work or family obligations should consider getting a pair of parakeets, because the birds will be happier with company. It doesn't matter if the two birds are of

Affectionate touching and rubbing of bills is the first step toward lifelong marriage or friendship. Put into words, it means something like "I'm here; please stay with me."

the same sex because one of them will in time assume the role of the missing gender. You will have the pleasure of watching the elaborate rituals of two parakeets linked by a permanent pair bond. It is even more exciting, of course, if you have a true pair that may actually mate. Such a pair may produce offspring, a subject covered in a separate chapter (see page 65).

Plumage Colors

The Australian ancestors of our domestically bred parakeets are all light green with a yellow face and forehead. This yellow area, which extends downward to the breast, where there are six black dots, is called the mask. There are also some violet-blue feathers on the sides of the face forming the cheek patches, which are still present in many of the cultivated strains. The back of the head, nape, back, and wing coverts are covered with wavy lines made up of feathers with black and yellow edges. The bill is beige; the cere is blue in males and beige to brownish in females.

Birds bred in captivity only rarely preserve the wild coloring; colors like olive green, dark green, sky blue, dark blue, violet, gray, yellow, white, and combinations like clearwings or greywings, predominate. Breeders have come up with special names for certain markings; thus, birds in which the color of the face mask extends over the head and upper back, forming a V between the markings of the wings, are

Raising both wings simultaneously can mean "I'm glad you're back" in parakeet language. Or it can be a way to cool down the body.

called "opalines." "Lutinos" are pure yellow with black or red eyes, and "albinos" are white with red eyes. There are also special creations such as the "round crest."

Tip: The strains that have the least in common with the original wild parakeet are the most likely to succumb to sickness. Perhaps this hint will help you choose the right kind of bird.

Cage Placement

A pet parakeet's cage is its refuge, the place where it feels safe. The cage is its territory and private space, where even the most familiar human should not intrude unnecessarily. In its cage the bird can rest, recover from any fright it may have sustained, eat in peace, and sleep. To serve as such a secure home base, the cage should have a permanent place.

The living room is the best location for the cage; there the parakeet gets a chance to see the whole family most often. Place the cage in a corner, if possible, and near a window, on a

(opposite page, top) The original coloration of parakeets is light green with a yellow mask and wavy black-and-yellow shell markings on the back of the head, the upper back, and the wing coverts. All the other colors are the result of selective breeding.

(opposite page, bottom) A trio of blue parakeets.

(top left) This is a white-winged blue parakeet.

(top right) Green with a yellow face and forehead.

(left) There are many color varieties from which to choose.

shelf that is attached securely to the wall. The shelf should be at a height from which the bird can look at the faces of the people in the room. Parakeets are happiest if they can watch their humans' faces. There should be nothing above the cage because parakeets get frightened by activity over their heads.

Important: The location of the cage should be absolutely free from drafts because drafts will lead to illness. Check for drafts with a lit candle. Even a draft too slight for us to notice will set the flame flickering.

Inappropriate Locations

You should avoid putting the cage in the following places:

✔ Directly in front of a window: It's too cold in the winter and too hot in the summer.

✔ The kitchen: Too many dangers—harmful vapors, hot burners, pots and pans with liquid or hot contents, cleansers and other chemicals that are toxic for the bird. Also, it's too drafty when the kitchen has to be aired.

✔ A child's room: Life here is too boring because children spend most of the day in school, playing, doing sports, going to the movies, and doing homework. And then they have to go to sleep.

Other Location Problems

With air conditioning common in many homes, you must also consider resolving the problem of having the parakeet in the same room that is being air cooled. The problem can be avoided by locating the bird's cage in a room that is not air conditioned as long as that room is not inappropriate for the reasons mentioned earlier. If you have the entire house air conditioned, you can locate the bird in a room

that is not as cool as the other parts of the house. If the flow of cooled air is strong, you must not permit it to blow directly on the bird's cage. You can actually deflect the flow of air by setting up a simple barrier made of cardboard or you can use a free-standing screen, which will be more attractive.

Your parakeet will tend to follow your lifestyle in terms of going to bed and waking up. Since the bird needs seven to eight hours of regular sleep, you will be keeping it awake when it should be sleeping if you watch TV in the cage area or have visiting friends in that room who are engaging in conversation or noisy activities.

If your living quarters do not permit you to locate the bird in a more peaceful and quiet room, you can utilize a cage cover that will block light, noise, and the bird's view of the activities going on in the room. This is not a perfect solution, but it will permit the parakeet to sleep even if it is in a room where people are active.

Many times during the day you will notice your parakeet dozing with its head turned and its beak nestled in its shoulder or back feathers. This is not abnormal. Many pets tend to doze during the day.

A Change of Scene

As the cold, gray days of winter change to the lovely mild weather and balmy breezes of spring and summer, many people begin to spend more time outside. Devoted pet owners are often tempted to bring their parakeets out of the house so that they too can enjoy the mild weather. There is nothing wrong with doing this if you follow certain precautions.

Even if your parakeet's wings are clipped, you should never let it climb or fly freely outside because parakeets can jump, climb, and even flutter out of your reach. If you read the lost-and-found ads in your local newspaper during the spring and summer months, you will find many plaintive ads from owners seeking their lost parakeets, parrots, and cockatiels who "flew the coop."

The best way to bring your bird outside is in a cage. This can be its regular cage or a spare that you keep just for this purpose. Be sure not to place the cage in direct sunlight for more than a short period of time. You can keep your parakeet in a sundappled area under a tree for a longer time. It is not wise to leave the cage alone because other pets or wild birds may investigate and frighten your parakeet.

As a special treat, you can carefully slide out the tray of the cage and the metal plate below it so that your parakeet is in direct contact with the grass. (Choose an area that has not been chemically treated with fertilizer or weed killer.) You can even dig up a small section of turf so that the bird will be able to continue the activity that you have started. Of course you must keep an eye on your bird during this time to be sure that it does not ingest too much of the grass and earth.

If the weather permits, this is also a good time to give your parakeet a light sprinkle with tepid water from a plant mister. You can do this right through the bars of the cage, but take out the food dish first if you have one in this outdoor cage. Most parakeets will spread their wings to catch as much water as possible when you do this. If done regularly during warm summer days, you will find that your parakeet's feathers assume a beautiful luster from the regular sprinkling. Avoid the temptation to use a garden hose for this activity. Its stream is too powerful and the water coming from the hose is much too cold for the parakeet.

PURCHASE TIPS

Where to Buy Parakeets

Pet stores sell parakeets in many colors. You can also buy everything you need to outfit the cage there.

Breeders, too, have parakeets for sale. Get addresses from bird breeders' clubs (see Information on page 83), perhaps from an animal shelter, or from your local veterinarian.

Tip: Take plenty of time to observe the parakeets offered for sale; perhaps one of them will appeal to you more than the others because it is so active and playful, or because it looks at you with curious eyes, or because you like its colors, or for some other reason. If you spontaneously find the parakeet that is right for you, then the sex doesn't matter.

Important Considerations

Age of the bird at purchase: The parakeet you buy should be young, about five weeks old; at this age it will get used to people and a new environment quickly. It should also be healthy so that you can enjoy it for a long time and it will be a good learner.

Hand-taming your parakeet is possible with a great deal of patience; using spray millet also helps.

How to recognize a young parakeet:
✔ It has big, black button eyes, in which the white iris is not yet visible.
✔ The wavy barring still extends over the entire head, all the way down to the cere, which doesn't turn blue in males until after the prenuptial molt.

What a healthy parakeet looks like:
✔ All the feathers are fully formed; they are lustrous and lie smooth against the body.
✔ The feathers around the vent—the anal opening of a bird—are not sticky or dirty with fecal matter.
✔ There is no discharge from the eyes and nostrils, nor are they encrusted with old, dried-up secretions.
✔ The horny scales on the feet and toes form a smooth surface.
✔ On each foot there are two toes pointing forward and two pointing backward. No toes should be missing.
✔ The bird moves quickly, grooms itself frequently, and has active contact with its fellows.

The sick parakeet: It sits apathetically in a corner, its plumage ruffled and its eyes half shut, the bill tucked into the back feathers. If you see a bird like this, take a second look a little while later; perhaps it was just napping.

For many parakeets, a little bell is an indispensable toy that helps pass the time on the occasions when they have to be left alone.

The Cage

Keep in mind when you buy the cage that the future home of your parakeet should not be a prison but a safe refuge and a place for eating and sleeping. The cage should be large enough so that the bird can spread its wings and at least go through the motions of using them. Even if you are determined to keep your

parakeet in a cage that has the cage door open most of the time, the bird will still, for its own good, have to spend many hours in the closed cage (when you air the room, clean, have family gatherings, and so on).

Tip: Buy your parakeet's cage early enough so that it will be completely set up and ready for the bird's arrival.

Stands for hanging bird cages are sold by pet supply stores in various designs. They are usually made of metal, are heavy at the bottom, and have a hook at the top from which the cage is hung. This kind of stand makes it easier to move the cage when that seems desirable.

Warning: Because the heavy bottom is usually attached to the top part with a screw, the screw can work itself loose, thus endangering the stand's stability. Check the connection periodically and tighten the screw, if necessary. Sometimes the cage bottom suddenly drops away from the wire part of the cage because the clamps connecting top and bottom are not gripping solidly enough and they may let go. To prevent such an accident, use a wide rubber band to hold the cage together.

Cage Description

Ideal dimensions: 40 by 20 by 32 inches (100 × 50 × 80 cm).

Minimum dimensions: 20 by 12 by 18 inches (50 × 30 × 45 cm).

Bars: Horizontal on the long sides so that the bird can climb up on them.

Perches: Made of wood and of different

Depending on its mood, a parakeet regards its reflection in the mirror as either a partner or a rival. This imagined companion can provide consolation during lonely hours.

thicknesses ($\frac{1}{2}$ and $\frac{3}{4}$ inches [12 and 20 mm]). The bird's toes should not reach all the way around the perches.

Bottom pan: Made of plastic.

Sand drawer: Should slide in and out.

Food dishes: Two—one for grain, the other for water.

Swing: Usually included in the cage.

Tip: Replace the perches that come with the cage with natural branches of various thicknesses (diameters are given on page 14). For types of wood to choose, see A Bird Tree, pages 30–32. These branches are not only wonderful to climb on but also provide work for the bird's bill.

A cage with the minimum dimensions can be used only as a place for the bird to eat and sleep in. For living, a parakeet with such a small cage needs a play area, namely a bird tree.

So-called indoor aviaries: These are sold by pet supply firms and are useful for a pair of birds that you hope to breed, but they are not large enough to serve as flight areas. For that, parakeets need much more space.

Tip: No matter how large its cage, a parakeet still needs a daily session of flying free (see page 29).

The Band

When you buy a parakeet, it may have a band on its leg that identifies the breeder. You should check the banded leg frequently, because bands can cause problems. If the band gets caught on something, for instance, the bird will try to yank its leg free and may injure itself. If the leg then swells up, the band hinders the blood flow. In that case, the band should be removed by an experienced parakeet breeder or your avian veterinarian. Keep the band for future reference.

Other Needs

Before you set out to get your parakeet at the pet store or at the breeder's, make a list of all the things you still would like to get for your bird.

Shopping List

✔ Mixed birdseed, preferably the kind the parakeet is used to.

✔ A spray of millet. Millet sprays are a favorite treat and are also highly nutritious (see Enriching the Diet, page 50).

✔ A stone for sharpening the bill. When you buy one, look for a note on the package saying something like: "Mineral stone containing all elements necessary for healthy bones and for the formation of feathers."

✔ A bathhouse. This is hung in the opened cage door and should have a textured floor so that the bird won't slip when taking a bath.

✔ One or two extra food dishes to be hung on the cage bars for fruit, vegetables, and sprouted seeds.

✔ Some kind of automatic water dispenser. Water supplied in a water bottle hung upside down in the cage will not get dirty the way it does in a dish.

✔ Toys, such as a small mirror or a little bell that is hung in the cage. These toys provide some distraction and consolation after the parakeet's separation from its fellows.

✔ Bird sand for the floor of the cage. The sand not only serves a sanitary function but also contributes to the bird's health (see page 42).

Five parakeets sitting on their wooden cage perch.

Two parakeets affectionately rubbing bills.

A young blue and an adult green share a perch.

Two colorful male parakeets, one green, one blue.

Beyond the Basics

The number of toys made for parakeets is rather limited and these toys do not always take the true nature of the parakeet into consideration. If you are ambitious, you can make some excellent toys that will provide long-term fun for your bird.

Types of Toys

Toys for a parakeet fall into several categories. The first of these is toys that make noise. These are generally very popular with parakeets. Although small bells can be purchased at your pet store, they usually make only a tinkling sound and there is also some danger. If the bell is poorly constructed, your bird might be able to remove the clapper. If the clapper is small enough, it can be swallowed, and if it is made of lead (as some foreign imports are), it represents a poisoning menace if the parakeet chews the soft metal.

A homemade toy: You can use a small but heavy spoon, such as a demitasse spoon or a spoon that is made for a child. Drill a hole in the handle about halfway down toward the bowl of the spoon, and attach it to the cage with a leather thong. The thong must be thick enough so that it cannot be twisted to form a noose.

Don't be alarmed if your bird doesn't use its new toy right away. Your parakeet has to make sure that the spoon is not an enemy. After a short period of time, your parakeet will swing it and spin it so that it bangs against the cage bars, making a very pleasing noise.

Making a chew toy: Parakeets love to chew. In the wild, they engage in plenty of chewing activities that may ultimately culminate in the chewing of an existing tree cavity so that it becomes a nest. Most of the toys that you buy for your bird are designed to be long lasting, and, thus, they are not particularly chewable.

Visit your local lumber yard and get permission to collect a bag of scrap pine. Even if you have to pay a small fee for this wood, you will be able to make future toys from it that will be well worth whatever the wood may cost. Be sure to choose only unstained pieces of wood and avoid those with nails or other foreign objects embedded in them. For your purposes, choose scraps of wood that are only about one inch (2.5 cm) thick. When you get the wood home, be sure to check more thoroughly for nails, brads, and so forth, and remove any that you may find.

The wood may then be cut into pieces. Drill several holes in the wood pieces so that your bird will not find it too difficult to get started on chewing them. Hang a piece of the wood from a leather thong (using the same caution described previously) and you will find that your parakeet will chew the wood until only splinters remain.

If you have access to a willow tree that has not been sprayed with any chemicals, you can also cut finger-sized pieces of willow twigs from the branches. If necessary, pull on the lower end of a flexible branch to bring it closer to you and snip off a good-sized piece of the branch using pruning shears. Your bird will delight in these twigs and will usually first remove the bark in one or two slippery pieces and then chew the remaining wood to bits.

The Joy of Music

A source of music is another item to add to your shopping list. Animal behaviorists and veterinarians have become aware of pet stress and separation anxiety problems caused by the daily departure of the beloved owner from the home. Tapes or CDs with appropriate music created to soothe as well as to be enjoyed are now available in your pet store at a nominal price. You will probably find that the music is so soothing that you will also enjoy listening to it when you are in your bird's room.

GRADUAL ADJUSTMENT

The New Home

Pack your parakeet in a small carrying box and bring it home as quickly as possible, protecting it, of course, from cold, dampness, and excessive heat. You want the bird to get used to its new home and quickly get over the sadness of being separated from its siblings. You hope that it will soon overcome its fear of the new, unfamiliar surroundings and come to regard the people with whom it is now living as surrogate partners. At the beginning, at least, the cage will be the bird's immediate home and refuge. If possible, you should have it all set up before you go out to buy your bird so that no major last-minute changes will have to be made. Final touches can be added at the very last minute just before you release your parakeet from its carrying box.

Arranging the Cage

Remove any plastic perches; it is best to replace them with natural branches cut to the right length. Either stick them between the bars or tie them in place with string made of raffia.

The new member of the household will need time to adjust to its new and strange surroundings.

✔ Don't put in more branches than there were perches.

✔ Three branches should be placed horizontally, and one or two at an angle; after all, the branches birds perch on in nature are not all horizontal.

✔ Spread bird sand about ½ inch (1 cm) deep in the tray at the bottom of the cage.

✔ Fill one dish with some mixed birdseed, pour water in another, and put pieces of peeled apple and some grated carrot in a third.

✔ Fasten a spray of millet to the cage bars near one of the branches, using a clothespin or a special clip (available at pet stores).

✔ Hang the bell from one of the higher branches, and fasten the mirror to the cage in such a way that the bird can see itself when sitting on one of the branches.

Tip: Keep raffia on hand for the birds to gnaw on; replace it from time to time.

The First Few Hours

When you hold the opened carrying box against the open cage door, your parakeet is almost certain to emerge from the darkness of the box and move toward the light.

Important: Close the cage door as soon as the bird is inside, and move away.

For the next few hours you should refrain from reaching into the cage. Give your parakeet time to examine its new surroundings in peace from the preferably somewhat elevated position of its cage, but stay in the same room and talk to the bird. Say the name you have chosen for it frequently. You will soon notice that the parakeet begins to react to the name, perhaps responding with a sound or with a movement. If it eats a few seeds, or pecks at some of the fresh food, this is a sign that the worst shock is over.

Night Rest

Bedtime comes when you dim the light in the evening and turn down the sound of the TV. Television will not bother the bird if the screen is not directly in its line of vision; if there is any question in your mind, you can drape a light cloth over the cage. The parakeet may still tweet for a while, but it will gradually get drowsy and fall asleep. Leave a small light on for the first few nights; if the bird is startled by an unfamiliar noise, it may panic and start flapping wildly. Once it realizes it is in its usual surroundings, it is likely to calm down again.

Once it has gotten used to its new life, the parakeet will choose a specific, permanent spot for sleeping. It might perch on the swing, favor a certain corner of the cage, or cling to the cage bars near the bell. If the bird has developed this habit, you have to make sure your parakeet has settled down in its sleeping place before you turn out the lights. If it is in the wrong place, the bird will not sleep well.

Developing Trust

Fear can be a paralyzing, all-consuming feeling, and for as small a creature as a parakeet, there are plenty of things around that inspire fear and terror. That is why you should be especially careful during the first few weeks to shield your new parakeet from getting frightened—the more pleasant its first experiences are and the more self-confidence the bird gains in its new environment, the easier it will be for you to later deal with potentially frightening situations.

To help your parakeet learn to trust you:
✔ Speak to the bird soothingly whenever you have to reach into the cage in the course of the daily cleaning. Say its name a lot, praise it, or sing to it—always the same song. Your voice and tone of voice will have a reassuring effect.
✔ Don't be startled if the young bird pecks at your hand; it won't have developed enough courage yet to bite hard.
✔ Avoid abrupt, hasty movements.
✔ Try to do the routine cleaning chores at the same time every day.

What Upsets Parakeets

Parakeets are creatures of habit and suspicious of anything that looks different. This fear of change extends to all objects inside the cage as well as to things in the immediate and wider surroundings, and it includes your external appearance. So don't suddenly put a food dish in a different spot, introduce a new toy, or come up to the cage wearing curlers, a black hat, or some other unusual and conspicuous

The perches inside the cage and on the bird tree have to be thick enough so that the bird's toes don't reach all the way around.

The craving for spray millet makes many parakeets forget their fear of the human hand. If your parakeet feels for a toehold on your finger, you've almost won the game.

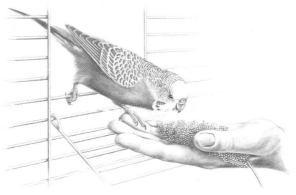

item of clothing. Parakeets also initially regard the human hand as a dangerous or even life-threatening object. They get used to it only gradually and if it is not associated with any frightening experiences. It is therefore important to avoid reaching for a bird that is still shy; all birds are terrified if grasped. Only a bird that is tame and has learned to trust you may be picked up in an emergency.

Getting Birds Used to New Things

A bird has to be introduced very gradually to anything new, no matter how small and insignificant it may seem. You may have to offer a certain fruit or vegetable it has not had before for quite a while before the bird will dare taste it.

A new lamp first has to be set up quite far away from the cage and moved just a little bit closer every day before the parakeet accepts it as part of its surroundings. A new toy may also be perceived as a threat. Any unaccustomed or frightening activities or loud noises, such as blowing your nose or vacuuming, should at first always be accompanied by the same soothing words. I used to warn Manky, a real "scaredy-cat" of a parakeet, every time before I blew my nose. "Excuse me, but I have to blow my nose." Soon all I had to do was to take out a handkerchief, and Manky would promptly comment by saying the same sentence.

Hand-taming

Once your parakeet has adjusted to its new home, has lost some of the fear of the first days, and has become a little more trusting through daily interaction with you, you can start to get it used to your hand. Follow these steps:

1. Stop sticking spray millet between the bars and offer it instead from your hand inside the cage every day at the same time. At first the bird will probably not dare to get close enough to your hand to peck at the millet, but will only eye it briefly and then look away. Remain motionless and talk softly to the bird.

2. Perhaps as early as the second day, your parakeet will try—from as far away as possible and craning its neck full length—to peck a few grains off the millet spray, or your efforts may go unrewarded for days on end. At some point, however, the parakeet will muster enough courage to try its luck. Just keep offering the millet every day with the same patience and calmness. Soon your hand will look as familiar to your parakeet as the millet spray, and one day the bird will get up on your finger to reach

A young parakeet eats from a feed tray inside its cage.

better, while resting on one foot only; the other one is kept on the perch just to be on the safe side.

3. Don't lose patience. Eventually, the bird will accept your entire hand to perch on, and not just for eating. Soon it will also hop onto your hand to be taken out of the cage and put back in.

Tip: Always offer the back of your hand for the bird to perch on. Many birds are afraid of an open hand.

Warning: Never grab a bird except in a real emergency, and never try to catch it in flight! There is no worse terror for a bird than being grasped. Such an experience could ruin the trust in the human hand the bird has developed (see What Upsets Parakeets, page 22).

Note the scaling on the forehead of this young blue parakeet.

Your bird will need time to shed its shyness before it responds to your acts of friendship.

HOW-TO: BATHING

If one day you find your parakeet dancing around the water dish and pecking at it, or if it is trying to dip its abdomen into the water, this is a clear sign that the bird would like to bathe. At this point you can fill the bathhouse with about 3/4 inches (2 cm) of lukewarm water and hang it inside the cage door opening. If the desire for a bath outweighs the distrust of the unfamiliar bathhouse, the bird will immediately perch on the tub's edge and start out by taking a few sips of the water.

A Full Bath

After tasting the water, the bird will step into the water, trembling slightly, lower its abdomen into it, and try to dunk first one spread wing, then the other. Unfortunately, the bathhouse is too small for

this. Later, when it has become quite tame, you can offer your parakeet a large flowerpot saucer to bathe in, where it can dip at least one wing at a time into the water. But for the beginning, a bathhouse will do.

A Dew Bath

If your bird doesn't dare approach the bathhouse, even though it has expressed a desire for bathing, hang the bathhouse in the cage every day from now on, so that the bird can get used to it. You can also rinse some parsley, young dandelion greens, chickweed, or spinach in water and place them with some of the moisture still on them, in the bathhouse. Many parakeets prefer this kind of "dew bath." After all, they are birds that live on the steppes in nature, where they bathe in

the dewy grass while foraging for food in the morning.

Tip: Don't use any vegetables that have been sprayed with chemicals. The chemicals dissolve in the water and can prove harmful to the bird.

A Shower Bath

If your parakeet doesn't overcome its distrust of the bathhouse, try giving it showers with a plant mister. The bird doesn't need to be sprayed until it is dripping wet; it merely has to have a chance to get some moisture on its feathers. If it enjoys this "shower," it will turn around, in the spray, exposing all parts of its body to the fine mist. If, on the other hand, it acts frightened and tries to get away, wait until it once more exhibits an interest in bathing and then offer the bathhouse or a shower again. Don't give up after a few tries; remember that it takes parakeets time to get used to new experiences.

Important: Make sure the spray bottle you are using for the shower is new and rinse it thoroughly before using it.

Other Bathing Tips

You may find that your parakeet prefers to bathe by

A big flowerpot saucer is spacious enough to allow a parakeet to submerge its wings in the water. The bird will probably soon prefer it to a bathhouse.

dipping its head and beak into the water dish and then vigorously flinging the water back over its shoulder onto the rest of its body. Although a fine bath can be had in this way, it is not as sanitary as using a dish meant for bathing. Try to encourage your bird to use its bathhouse or the dish that you have provided specifically for bathing.

In addition to placing greens in the bath dish to attract the parakeet, you can also place them on top of the bird's cage when they are dripping wet after rinsing. Most parakeets will check to see what these objects are and then attempt to pull the tasty greens into the cage to eat them. The result will be a delicious shower.

When using the spray bottle technique, you can use water that is quite warm. You will find that as it passes through the air, it cools down before it reaches the parakeet and it will be at a comfortable temperature for your bird. Of course, it is vital that you test the water on your own hand or wrist first to make sure that it is comfortable enough for the bird.

Some bird owners (particularly those who intend to show their birds at contests) like to add a small amount of glycerin to the water

It takes time for a parakeet to get used to a bathhouse. Hang it in the opening of the cage door with some water or wet herbs on the bottom.

that they spray on their birds. Although this will add luster to the feathers, it is not an absolutely necessary routine for the average pet parakeet owner to follow.

If you look at the advertisements in the various bird magazines (see page 83), you will see "shower perches" offered for birds. These devices make it possible for your parakeet to bathe in the shower with you. However, I would not recommend this activity, because there is always the risk of you slipping or falling against your bird and causing an injury. Your bird can play with you, eat with you, watch TV with you, but it might be best to let your bird shower alone.

DAILY CARE

Flying Free

During the period when your parakeet is getting acclimated, please don't get the impression that from now on you will have to behave as though you were walking on eggshells when you are home. This kind of caution is necessary only during the first few days, or perhaps for the first two to three weeks, depending on your bird's temperament. Even during this initial phase you will experience many happy moments of success. One morning your parakeet will show its pleasure at seeing you and shake its plumage vigorously. It will start to respond to your greetings or whistled tunes by tweeting back cheerfully, or it may display its trusting mood by setting the bell ringing while you are still cleaning the cage. These are all indications that your parakeet is getting more and more interested in its new world and would like to explore a wider territory. The best way to satisfy this desire is to let the bird fly free in the room, but to make sure that your bird won't encounter any mishaps and can enjoy flying free without constant supervision, I would like to recommend a few useful procedures based on my own experience.

When you allow your parakeet to fly free, you never know what it will find fascinating, such as this woven basket.

Flying Without Risks

A parakeet gets to know its new environment best and most quickly if it can fly around in it often and for extended periods of time. This not only helps a bird feel comfortable in its new surroundings but is also good for its health, but before you open the cage, close all doors and windows in the room and draw the window curtains. Since birds don't recognize glass as a barrier, your parakeet might crash against a window with full force and injure or even kill itself. One way to get a parakeet used to curtainless windows is to lower shades all but about 8 inches (20 cm), turning on the light if it gets too dark in the room. Then increase the uncovered part of the windows a little bit every day until the bird has learned to regard windows as a barrier. Usually this takes only a few days. If the room has large glass sliding doors, put several decals on the doors to alert the bird to the doors' presence.

The First Flight

If at first your parakeet just sits inside the cage, staring through the open cage door as though hypnotized, and doesn't immediately launch itself into the free air, don't worry. Remember that it probably has never before had a chance to fly; in the nest box there wasn't enough room, and in the communal cage it probably couldn't do much more than flutter its wings.

At some point it won't be able to resist the temptation to take a closer look at the room it sees beyond the open rectangle; perhaps it will first climb on top of the cage. But soon the urge to fly will overcome fear, and your parakeet will take to its wings and cross the room for the first time.

Landing maneuvers: Flying itself presents no problems, but landing may be a different story—first of all because your bird probably has never done it before, and second, because there are so many unfamiliar, fear-inspiring things in the room. With some luck, the bird may be able to land on the cage. If that is the case, leave it up to your parakeet whether it wants to have another go at it or whether it prefers to retreat to the safety of the cage. The next day it will go about flying with much less hesitation.

How to lure the bird back into the cage: If your parakeet lands on the floor, put down some birdseed for it; parakeets love to forage for food on the ground. Then, when you place the cage near it a little bit later, the bird will probably be happy to climb back in. Should your bird land on a bookcase, a lamp, or a curtain rod, the return flight becomes a test of courage. The higher the spot where it has landed, the safer the bird feels. This feeling is instinctive because in nature a high perch usually means greater safety from predators—and now it is afraid to abandon this place of refuge. Overcoming the reluctance is a major struggle and takes time. Talk to the bird, and try to lure it off its perch with a spray of millet. If this doesn't work, hold the open cage up to the bird after about half an hour. Perhaps it will step into it, relieved; if not, leave the bird sitting where it is. It will manage a safe return eventually, even if not until the next morning.

Warning: Don't even consider chasing the bird or trying to dislodge it by waving a piece of cloth at it. This sort of thing would destroy all the trust the bird has developed.

A Bird Tree

Once my first parakeet discovered how much more fun it was to sit outside the cage rather than in it, it took to spending almost the entire day outside the cage. It would fly through the room now and then, but always landed on the cage and watch me work at my desk. Whenever I left it alone, it would seek refuge on the indoor linden *(Sparmannia africana)*. But the plant's branches were much too thin to make good perches, so I attached some natural branches to the tree for the bird to sit on. Now the linden tree became the parakeet's favorite

A parakeet is so flexible that it can reach all parts of the body with its bill when preening its plumage.

spot, but when a second parakeet joined our household, the plant did not survive for long. The two parakeets loved to nip off branches and let the leaves sail down to the floor. At this point, I decided to buy a large tub of the kind used for hydroculture and I built my first bird tree. This artificial tree became—and for many years remained—a haven of delight for my birds in the middle of my study.

Of course, the branches of such a tree and the raffia strings tying them together have to be replaced every few months, but when I watched the delight with which my birds nibbled on the branches, the time and effort spent seemed well worthwhile. You do, however, have to be careful about what branches to pick.

Nonpoisonous Branches

Fruit tree branches are ideal, but only if you are absolutely sure that they haven't been sprayed. If you have the slightest doubt, it is better to pick branches from other trees, such as oak, alder, elderberry, chestnut, basswood, poplar, or willow. Even here you have to be careful: Don't gather them near roads and highways because everything there is contaminated with chemicals from car emissions, and these poisonous substances are absorbed by the wood. Even branches from parks and from woods should be hosed off with hot water and let dry before a bird touches them, as even parks are not safe from harmful substances, and acid rain falls everywhere.

Constructing a Bird Tree

✔ Put a few heavy stones in the bottom of a large flowerpot or tub to lend stability.
✔ In the middle of this pot place a smaller flowerpot with a *nonpoisonous* vine.

✔ Use wire to attach three or four branches or bamboo sticks about 6 feet (2 m) long and 1¼ inches (3 cm) thick vertically to the smaller pot.
✔ Fill the space between the smaller pot and the edge of the larger one with earth, and top with bird sand.
✔ Now connect the vertical branches with natural branches ½ to ¾ inches (12–20 mm) thick to form several "floors," tying the horizontal branches to the vertical sticks with raffia string. Not all these connecting branches have to be absolutely horizontal; after all, the bird is supposed to do a lot of climbing in the tree.
✔ Tie a little bell and a mirror to different branches in such a way that they are at eye level with the bird when it sits on a branch. The best place is near a forked branch, as parakeets like to perch on forked branches.
✔ Replace the branches and the string, as well as the branches in the cage, every few weeks.

Tip: Check to see that the perching branches don't stick out beyond the rim of the larger tub. If they do, some of the droppings will land on the floor instead of in the bird sand.

Where to Put the Tree

Needless to say, the bird tree needs a permanent spot in the room. It is best if it is placed at some distance from the cage, because then the bird is forced to fly back and forth several times a day. While a parakeet is young and full of energy, it needs no special urging to fly, but as it gets older and perhaps a little lazier, having to fly to and from the tree is a good counterbalance to a sedentary way of life. It should also go without saying that food and water are offered in the cage only; otherwise, the bird

may be tempted not to bother flying back at all. A good place for the bird tree is next to a window, where the parakeet can watch birds

This blue adult male enjoys perching on its branch. Be sure to use only nonpoisonous branches that will not harm your pet.

flying outside and where there is plenty of light during the day.

A Bird-proof Room

Probably no bird-keeper, no matter how conscientious, will succeed in eliminating all sources of danger that lurk in a room inhabited by both birds and humans. I have all too often seen these small, agile avian creatures discover fascinating things we humans are quite oblivious of. One time, when she was getting ready to brood, my female parakeet Clowny was suc-

These two parakeets have stopped for a rest during a free-flight outing from their cage.

Make sure that your parakeets have plenty of stimulating toys to keep them occupied.

cessful in squeezing through a space about 1¼ inches (3 cm) wide between the ceiling and a bowl-shaped glass ceiling lamp. The lamp was smooth on the outside, but on the inside the glass had veins with knife-sharp edges. By the time we had freed her, her feet were bloody. Nevertheless, she renewed her efforts to nest there until we stuffed the space between ceiling and lamp with rags. Another incident spurred me on to renew my vigilance in bird-proofing the room: When I came home one day, I found all the birds but one in their favorite places. Only the youngest, Sibyll, was nowhere to be seen. I couldn't imagine where she might be and looked in all conceivable hiding places—in vain. Then a soft rustling in the wastebasket caught my attention. Sibyll had probably slipped off the rim of the basket and once she had fallen in, could not get out of this smooth "tube" without help.

The Danger of Escape

Many pet parakeets escape at some point. Keep in mind that in the climatic conditions in various parts of the country, the birds have no chance of survival. To make things worse, para-keets are unable to make use of striking land-marks to help them orient themselves. It is an ability they have no need for in their original nomadic life in Australia. That is why a lost parakeet almost never finds its way back home and will die unless it happens to be found and taken in by someone. For these reasons, the first and foremost rule for any parakeet owner is to keep doors and windows closed at all times. A parakeet can escape even from a closed cage by squeezing through the crack of the drawer opening if the sand tray is left out for a moment, or it may learn to open the cage door with its strong bill. Curtains in front of an open window offer no protection against escape either, because the bird can climb up on them, wend its way snakelike through the narrow space between curtain rings, and take off. That is why at least one window in the bird room should have a strong metal screen with spaces

Dangers for Your Parakeet

Dangers	*How to Avoid the Danger*
Bathroom: The bird flies out through an open window or drowns in the toilet bowl.	Make sure the bathroom door is always closed; let the bird in only when you are present.
Bookshelves: The bird hides behind books and cannot escape without your help.	Make sure that books are pushed flush against the wall; lay a few books flat at intervals.
Burning candles: The bird can be fatally burned if it flies through the flame.	Do not light candles when the bird flies free.
Closets and open drawers: The bird is inadvertently closed in and suffocates or possibly starves.	Do not leave closets and drawers open or even slightly ajar.
Containers filled with water: The bird falls into a bowl, a bucket, or a vase and drowns (soapsuds can be mistaken for a solid place for landing).	Make sure all containers are covered; don't let the bird out of its cage when you houseclean.
Direct sun; hot car: The bird can have heart failure caused by heatstroke.	Place the cage in shade; air the car.
Floor: The bird plays on the floor, where it can be accidentally stepped on, injured, and even killed.	Be extremely careful wherever you step.
Poisons: The bird can be fatally poisoned by alcohol, the lead in pencils, the points of magic markers and ballpoint pens, strong spices, adhesives, varnishes, glues, solvents, fertilizers, plastic wrap, cleansers, mercury, strong-smelling sprays, laundry detergents, and heavy cigarette smoke.	Make sure you store all of these substances and objects in a locked cabinet or a location where the bird cannot get at them.
Stovetop burners and electrical appliances: The bird can be fatally burned if it lands on a hot burner or appliance.	Keep pots with cold water on burners that are still hot; the bird should never fly unsupervised in the kitchen.
Temperature fluctuations: The bird can catch a cold or suffer heatstroke from abrupt changes.	Make sure the bird is accustomed to different temperatures in the range of 41 to 77°F (5–25°C).
Wastepaper baskets and ornamental vases: The bird can slide in and starve or die of heart failure because it feels trapped.	Either use woven wastebaskets or line the inside with wire mesh; fill vases with sand.

between the wires no larger than ³⁄₈ by ³⁄₈ inches (1 × 1 cm). The screen should be mounted on a wooden frame that fits tightly into the window opening. This way you won't have to worry about airing the room, and you can let the bird live in it without constant supervision.

Plants in the Bird Room

The plants to be kept in the bird room either for decoration or as a supplement to the bird tree also have to be chosen with care, as they can be a source of danger as well. Here is a list of ones to watch out for:

The bird should never be in contact with any of the following: poison primrose *(Primula obconica), Strychnos nux-vomica,* Amaryllis *(Amaryllis* species), crown-of-thorns, all dieffenbachia species, yew, hyacinth, azalea, boxwood, periwinkle *(Vinca minor),* all nightshades, such as coral plant *Jatropha multifida;* also, narcissus, oleander, yam bean berries of ardisia plants, poinsettia, variegated laurel *(Codiaeum variegatum),* mistletoe, the berries of ornamental asparagus, and datura.

While the following plants are not poisonous, they do contain substances that irritate the mucous membrane and can be quite harmful to such small creatures as birds: ivy, monstera, flamingo flower, Chinese evergreen, *Aglaonema,* philodendron, and schefflera.

Nonpoisonous house plants can, of course, be enjoyed by you and your bird; but it is

Pet birds need a place where they can spend time comfortably outside their cage. A bird tree with natural branches can become a beloved mini-environment for birds.

always possible that your parakeet will take a special liking to one or another of them and prune it lovingly with its beak until there is not much left of it.

Be especially careful with cacti of all kinds and other plants with thorny or prickly parts; the birds can hurt their eyes on them.

Important: When you buy new plants, ask about their compatibility with birds. New kinds of plants, not included in our list, are becoming available all the time.

Boredom Is Harmful

Anyone who has a pet parakeet should keep in mind that a bird simply can't live the kind of life it was meant to live in an apartment designed for human occupancy. Even a pair of birds don't have enough to do to keep them busy. They don't spend time and energy in the search for food, they are rarely if ever absorbed

A parakeet can put a whiffle ball like this to all kinds of uses, but it will be happiest if you join in the game.

in parental duties, the female doesn't have to claim and prepare a nest cavity, the male doesn't have to defend the nest site against rivals, and the birds don't even have to worry about predators. To be sure, wild birds are not active every minute from dawn to dusk and take short naps several times during the day, and the intensive grooming of the plumage takes up time; still, if there is no other incentive to play and work with the bill, even young parakeets quickly become bored. These spirited, highly energetic, and intelligent birds have to be able to play, and they need encouragement and inspiration from their human partners to put their talents to good use.

Popular Toys

For a parakeet, having a partner of its own species around is the ideal way to dispel boredom. But even two birds can't keep on reestab-

A mirror is an indispensable toy for a parakeet that is kept singly.

lishing their hierarchical positions indefinitely, and they are not always in a courtship mood. Parakeets spend a surprising amount of time picking away at fresh branches and playing with objects. These objects don't always necessarily have to be toys. Anything that makes the birds move around and is used by them in different ways is fine. In pet stores you will find the following toys for parakeets:

✔ Small bells. Birds like these especially because they are made of shiny metal in which the birds can see themselves.

✔ Mirrors that can be hung in the cage or are mounted on a weighted toy that always comes to rest with the mirror on top. Usually, parakeets spend a lot of time with such a mirror because they keep jabbing at their reflection, which they think is a rival bird, and then running away to keep from being bumped when the mirror swings back or pops up again. Parakeets catch on quickly to the behavior of the mirror and like spending time with their imaginary foe.

✔ Plastic birds. These can be clamped to a perch; some parakeets beat up such a plastic companion like a rival, while others try to feed it like a partner or like a hungry baby bird. To a male bird, it represents the missing female partner, and to a female, nestlings.

✔ Solid balls or whiffle balls with or without a bell inside. These are made of plastic. A bird can play properly with such a ball only if you join in the game.

Birds may find toys among your belongings, such as small wooden objects. These may have been bought at the pet store or they may simply be around and appeal to your bird's instinct for play. Quite often, too, a bird will pick an object to serve as a friend and surrogate partner and display passionate love toward it. This

*Your parakeet will spend many hours
preening its plumage when left alone
in its cage.*

may be a thimble, a marble, a tiny metal box,
a chess or other board-game figure, or a die. In
a bird clinic, I once observed a sick parakeet in
an isolation cage huddling as close as it could
get to a glass to find consolation in its misery.
I found out from the bird's owner that this
glass was very important and provided great
comfort to the bird in all kinds of situations.

Important: Toys are meant to give pleasure
to the bird and keep it occupied. You should
therefore give a great deal of thought to the
nature of any toys that you introduce into
the cage. Toys made of lightweight plastic are
not safe because the parakeet can destroy
them and ingest bits of plastic. If you give your
parakeet a bell with a poorly attached clapper,
the bird may remove the clapper from the bell
and swallow it. Never use string or even cord
to hang a toy; these can form a noose and
result in death. The best way to hang a toy is
by using a leather thong that is thick enough
so that it cannot be twisted into a noose, or by
using a lightweight chain that is large enough
so that the bird cannot catch its claws in the
chain and trap itself. All toys should be washed
from time to time with hot water.

Stimulating Play

To be able to cope with the various chal-
lenges and demands of life in the wild, parakeets are equipped with intelligence, physical
agility, and excellent flying skills. In the life of
a pet bird, most of this potential lies idle. A
physically and emotionally healthy parakeet

transmutes these native talents into curiosity,
interest in vocal mimicry, and inventive play.
It likes to make use of the toys described on
page 36 to occupy itself, but if a bird is left to
its own devices, its interest and enthusiasm
soon wane; it needs you to be able to play
properly. It likes to set a ball rolling or it may
shove it deliberately toward the edge of a
table, and when the ball drops to the floor, it
watches with interest. If you pick up the ball
and perhaps put it back in the middle of the
table, the parakeet will patter up to it enthusi-
astically to continue the game. A parakeet can
pick up a whiffle ball with a bell inside, lift it
high with its bill, carry it across the entire
table, and toss it at you. If you roll the ball
back toward the bird, it will either get out of
the way timidly or walk straight up to it to toss
it back. If you set a little bell swinging, the bird
will run after it, as though playing tag, to give
it another shove, and then quickly dodge as it
swings back.

For me the whiffle ball became something of an exercise machine. My parakeet Manky would hold the ball in his bill, sitting on the top branch of the bird tree, and toss it at me, but very often I had to bend to pick the ball up off the floor because the smart bird was clever enough to make me miss the ball.

Keeping Busy When Alone

Your parakeet will keep a sharp eye on you to figure out when you are ready to play. If it notices no such indication, it will turn to other activities. Grooming or preening its plumage alone takes up considerable time every day. No feather goes untended. With great skill the parakeet pulls each flight feather on the wings and the tail through its bill to free it from dust, smooth it, and oil it lightly. The same is done with the contour feather. To oil its plumage, the bird rubs its head over the oil gland at the base of the tail or picks up oil and distributes it with its bill. The acrobatic skill displayed in preening is amazing. Except for the head, which birds allow their partners to preen, there is no place on the body that is not reached by the bill.

Every so often, birds need to take short rests. They often assume their sleeping posture, nap or doze a little, and become completely oblivious of their surroundings; then they wake up again refreshed and ready for new action. They may nibble on branches or on houseplants within their reach, or they may go after papers, books, wallpaper, or posters with special gusto. But don't worry too much—these are often just phases. For the first few months I had parakeets, all my manuscripts had jagged edges, but after a while pecking at the papers lost its attraction, and the birds turned to my books. I was more finicky about books than manuscripts, so I hung sheets over my bookshelves. Eventually, the books too, lost their fascination, and for a long time the birds' interest focused on my rock collection, where they couldn't do much damage.

Important: Parakeets continually need new incentives to use their beaks. Be sure you always supply them with fresh branches, cuttlebone, and pumice or other stone for sharpening the bill.

Intimate Togetherness

Playing, working with its beak, and resting are not the only things a parakeet wants to do. The most precious minutes of the day for a bird are when it can perch on your finger or shoulder and listen to your voice. If it hears its name, musical tunes, or short sentences often

Raising itself to its full height, this bird has carried the ball across the table. If you are willing to play, a real game can now start.

enough, it may try to repeat them. If you begin to detect the first words in its chattering, it is worthwhile to patiently encourage this talent. The bird will listen, entranced, several times a day to all the words it can already pronounce and also to new ones. Perhaps your particular parakeet has more of a gift for whistling or for imitating other sounds. Don't be disappointed if this is the case. Indulge in daily chatting sessions anyway because the bird loves being very close to you.

The best way to get the birds' full and undivided attention is to be in a room that is absolutely quiet when the daylight begins to fade and when there is nothing to distract the bird. This is also the right moment to try scratching the bird's head very gently. A parakeet has to get used to this gradually because at first it is suspicious of your finger. Try with the tip of your little finger. Birds like being scratched best on the head and neck because they can't reach these areas with their bill. Once your bird realizes what you are trying to do, it will quickly lose its shyness and enjoy the scratching. In return, it will probably start "preening" your eyelashes, eyebrows, and skin very affectionately, nibbling away gently.

A Talent for Talking

Parakeets with a talent for talking will repeat many expressions they hear often, such as greetings, names, verbal interdictions, swear words, or the "hello" you use to answer the telephone. If you would like to teach your parakeet specific expressions, however, observe the following rules:

✔ In situations that recur regularly, always say the same, appropriate expression. Say "good

morning" when you first enter the room in the morning, "good night" before turning out the light in the evening, or "here's a treat" when you bring food.

✔ Always say the same short phrase—using the same speaking rhythm—whenever the bird looks at you expectantly.

✔ Sing or whistle short tunes to the bird several times a day.

✔ During your moments of closeness, repeat all the vocabulary the bird has already learned. Be sure to make time for these sessions of intimate togetherness at least once every day.

✔ Perhaps you can tape the bird's repertoire of phrases and other sounds. Play the tape for the bird when it has to stay by itself for a short time.

Manky, the most gifted talker of all my parakeets, always flopped down on his belly in front of the tape player and listened with rapture. He knew the sequence of everything on the tape by heart and always started the next phrase wherever I had paused for breath when recording.

Using Words Appropriately

Stories are often told about birds that respond to certain situations with appropriate expressions. Usually these birds are African grey parrots. Parakeets are capable of this feat too; thus my parakeet Jackele would often sit next to Clowny, cooing tenderly, and repeat over and over: "Clowny, I love you so much." Of course he had heard me say this, but he only said it to Clowny, never to me or to one of my other parakeets. Or when visitors came and asked Manky "Well, and who are you?" he would answer promptly "Manky Wolter of Planegg." During the summer, we often had

a visitor spend time with us—Maxi, a parakeet that ordinarily lived without the company of other birds. Maxi didn't quite know what to make of our birds, and liked flying free best when they were locked up. To give vent to their resentment, they would move around in their cages with such acrobatic twistings and turnings that I would soon let them out too. Then, whenever Manky got too close to Maxi, the latter would call out in great agitation "Lock him up, lock him up!" which was what the grandmother in Maxi's family, who was afraid of birds, always said.

Intelligence

Professor Otto König, an ethologist working in Vienna, reports that he succeeded in training birds to count. According to him, parakeets, like jackdaws, can count up to six, which they demonstrate by picking up seeds. Pigeons can count up to five, while common ravens, yellow-fronted Amazons, and African grey parrots get all the way to seven. In the course of daily interaction with your parakeet, you, too, will notice signs of intelligence in your bird. One example of intelligence is the way a bird will slip out of its cage in a flash as soon as it notices that you are about to close the cage door.

My parakeet Jojo's favorite toy used to be a two-colored whiffle ball with a little bell inside it. I always had several of these balls on hand, but he preferred one particular one and only played with that one. If I secretly substituted another, outwardly identical ball, he would refuse to play with it, visibly sad, and look for "his" ball every-where. If I gave it back to him together with four other balls, he would run up to his favorite ball excitedly and completely ignore the others.

Manky found a clever way to circumvent his species' instinctive inhibition of aggression against females of the species. He had a favorite spot on my desk in front of a small onyx box, where I sometimes gave him his favorite food, hulled oats. He would eat them there ecstatically, lying practically flat on his belly. If, occasionally, he found his mate Mini there eating "his" oats, he resorted to the fol-lowing trick: With pretended innocence he would try to engage me in playing with him, using one of the above-mentioned whiffle balls, but he would do his best to toss the ball not toward me, but at Mini, so that she would be driven away from the oats, a scheme that worked quite often.

If you take proper care when introducing a new bird, your parakeets will soon become the best of friends.

When Manky was still my only parakeet, he would intently watch everything I did. When I had to go away for a longer time than usual, he must have had some way of telling this from my preparations. He would then sit on his tree with his back to me. When I was finally ready to depart, he would fly at me with a scream and try to hide inside my collar. This made me feel so sorry for him that I soon brought Mini home to keep him company.

A Second Parakeet

At first I had my doubts about acquiring a second bird. Would Manky continue to be as friendly and affectionate with me when he had the constant company of another parakeet? Would he stop his charming talking? When I first introduced Mini to him, I held her in my two hands so that only her head was visible. Manky ran up to her and brutally yanked a feather from her head. Mini screamed, and I immediately took her away. Manky had probably reacted out of jealousy. The next day I set Mini, who was not yet able to fly, down on the floor in front of Manky. He looked at her briefly from the desk where he was perched, and he must have recognized how young she was. In any case, he immediately began to feed her and continued to do so until she was completely independent.

His relationship with me didn't change in any way, and Mini was simply included in the friendship. Manky never again reacted jealously to her, but he insisted that our play and chatting periods be continued. Mini's interest,

Birds bury their bills in their back feathers not only when they sleep at night, but also for short rests during the day.

a vacuum cleaner. It takes a little more time to maintain the hygienic conditions necessary for the bird to thrive. If these chores aren't performed regularly, the bird will get sick. The cage, the bird tree, and all the accessories have to be kept clean. The best way to proceed is to draw up a cleaning schedule:

however, was concentrated almost exclusively on the partner of her own species, and she regarded me more as someone to fall back on when needed, a friend one could count on when one found oneself in a tight spot.

Acclimating a Second Bird
✔ The sex of the second parakeet is immaterial. If the two birds turn out to be of the same sex, one of them will assume the role of the missing gender. However, the new bird should be of fledgling age so that the older one can respond to it by assuming a parental role.
✔ If possible, start out by housing the new bird by itself for a week, and spend a lot of time with it. This will help it overcome its timidity and fear of you.
✔ When you first bring the birds together, leave the cage door open; then they can get out of each other's way if the older bird doesn't accept the newcomer right away.

Hygiene
Like all pets, parakeets create some dirt, but what they leave behind is easily removed with

Schedule of Chores

Daily
✔ Use a scoop to remove the soiled sand in the cage bottom and in the tub with the bird tree. Top off with some fresh sand.
   Warning: The bird might escape through the crack when you take out the sand tray. To be on the safe side, plug the open slit with a book or a damp cloth.
✔ Empty all the dishes, and the water bottle, wash them out with hot water, dry well, and fill them again. Fill the seed dish about half way.
✔ Scrub dirty branches with sandpaper and wipe them with a damp cloth. Heavily soiled branches may be scraped with a linoleum knife.
✔ Check in the afternoon to see if there is enough birdseed left. If there are too many empty hulls, remove them with a small spoon. Don't try to blow them off the seeds, because this raises too much dust.

Weekly
✔ Wash out and dry the cage bottom and the sand tray. Use warm water.

✔ Wash the mirror and the bell with hot water and dry them.

✔ Discard leftover birdseed. Rinse all dishes in hot water, dry, and refill them.

Monthly

✔ In the bathtub, wash the entire cage down with hot water, scrubbing all parts with a brush. Then rub everything dry; let wooden items fully dry in the air.

✔ Replace gnawed branches in the cage and on the bird tree with fresh ones that have been washed in hot water and dried well.

Important: It is better not to use an automatic food dispenser because these feeders clog easily. If not enough seeds slide down, a bird can starve to death in front of a filled feeder. Don't use detergents or cleansers for cleaning; the chemicals in them are toxic to the birds. Clean water about 130°F (55°C) is quite adequate and presents no danger.

Care During Vacation

When you make vacation plans for yourself, you must also make appropriate arrangements for your pet parakeet.

If you intend to travel with your parakeet, there are some considerations to keep in mind. You cannot take your parakeet on a trip abroad because the entry regulations that apply to all members of the parrot family are far too strict.

You may take your parakeet on car trips, but you must make sure that your bird is not exposed to drafts and that the air conditioning does not blow directly on the bird, even during hot weather. Your bird also should not be exposed to direct sun. For overnight stays in hotels or at the home of friends or relatives, you should keep your bird locked inside its cage for safety. It is not advisable to take your parakeet to outdoor sites such as campgrounds, but locations such as vacation cottages can provide a homelike atmosphere that your bird might enjoy.

If you do not want to take your pet parakeet away on vacation, then the best alternative is to leave it at home in its familiar surroundings. For this, you must have a reliable caretaker to look after the bird and to talk and play with it once or twice a day.

Boarding

Boarding the bird, perhaps with friends or relatives is a possibility, but give the temporary bird-keepers exact instructions on the bird's needs and send along all the things your parakeet needs to be happy. Make sure that the bird will be able to fly free often in its temporary lodging.

Pet stores sometimes board parakeets for a small fee, but a bird will not be able to fly free there.

In case of illness: Should you have to go to the hospital, whether unexpectedly or for some planned treatment, I recommend that you choose one of the alternatives mentioned above: a caretaker or boarding with a bird-keeper or pet store. If you live alone, look for a reliable person to look after your bird before the need arises.

Tip: Animal shelters often have names and addresses of bird lovers who are willing to take in one or two birds for a vacation or in an emergency. Try to contact and get together with such a person before you need him or her so that arrangements can be made quickly if the need arises.

THE PROPER DIET

Diet in the Wild

In their Australian homeland parakeets feed on the seeds of different grasses and other plants. If they pass through arid regions in their continual search for food, they stay near watering places because they need drinking water to soften the dry grains in their crops. If all the streams and pools of water dry up, the birds move around on the ground in their early morning foraging and drink the dew hanging from the blades of grass. It has been shown that they also eat some fresh greens and pick up tiny grains of mineral-rich sand, which is needed for proper digestion. As soon as a rainy period starts, the parakeets get ready to breed, because in a few days the grass and herbs will sprout new shoots. These plants will also soon produce half-ripe seeds, a highly nutritious food needed both by breeding parents and baby birds; without these seeds, raising off-spring would be out of the question.

Seed—The Basic Staple

Well-balanced seed mixtures that make up the basic staple of the parakeets' diet have been developed through the knowledge of wild parakeets' feeding habits within their natural environment. These seed mixtures are primarily

This green parakeet sits on a branch of colorful flowers.

made up of several varieties of millet and canary grass seeds. Oats, linseed, and niger seed are among the substances that are then added to make a balanced mixture. Good commercial mixtures often contain thistle as well, and pet food companies also add iodine grains, which prevent the thyroid from becoming enlarged.

Important: Always look at the packing date when you buy birdseed. It is stamped on the package and should not be dated back more than about three months because we have no way of knowing how long the seed was stored before being packaged. All commercially available grains and seeds are harvested once a year and remain viable for one year, though they are edible for two if stored properly. But since the nutritive value gradually declines even if seeds are stored properly, you should test the viability of each package you open. If the seeds geminate, they are still high in nutritive value (see Directions for Sprouting Seeds, page 51).

If only a small portion of the seeds sprout, the mixture is useless and should not be fed to the bird.

Signs of Deterioration

✔ Rot: Rotting seeds have a strong odor; healthy seeds have no odor.
✔ Mildew: you can recognize mildew by the whitish-grayish fuzz on the seeds, but you have to look the seeds over very carefully to detect it.

Parakeets particularly enjoy picking up seeds from the floor, a habit that goes back to their wild ancestors, who foraged on the ground for all their food.

✔ Vermin: seeds that are clumped together and have cobweblike filaments emanating from them indicate vermin.

Storing Seeds Properly

If you have only one or two parakeets, a package of birdseed will last you several weeks. While using up a package, you should store the seeds in a dark, dry, and airy place, just like grain for your own consumption.

Correct way: Hang the seeds in an appropriate place in a bag made of natural fiber or plastic. Or store the seed in the refrigerator.

Incorrect way: Putting the seeds in a paper bag, an open can, or an open jar.

Daily Amount of Birdseed

✔ Put 2 teaspoonsful per bird into the seed cup every morning; if you use 2 cups, put 1 teaspoonful in each.

✔ Skim the empty husks off the top in the early afternoon because otherwise, your bird will not be able to get at the seeds underneath.

✔ If there are just a few seeds left in the cup in the evening, add half a teaspoonful more so that the bird will find something to eat first

thing in the morning, when it needs food for energy.

It is correct to make sure your bird always has sufficient food at its disposal: If you are delayed on your way home after work, a well-stocked seed cup is a real blessing.

It is wrong to try to keep a bird from getting fat by rationing the birdseed it gets. Birds have a very active metabolism and need small amounts of food frequently. They become overweight only if their diet is wrong, if they don't get enough exercise, or if they don't have enough to keep them busy. So avoid unnecessary, fattening treats, such as the hearts, bars, and so on, sold in pet stores, that are covered with seeds stuck on with sugar or honey.

Tip: Don't blow the empty seed husks out of the cup. This is messy if done inside and dangerous if done at an open window because your bird might escape.

Pellets

Some parakeet owners like to feed pellets to their birds because they provide a diet rich in nutrients, vitamins, and minerals. Unfortunately, most parakeets ignore pellets or drop them out of their dishes. If you want to encourage your bird to try them, purchase a high-quality pellet that is specially manufactured for parakeets and follow the feeding instructions on the package.

Drinking Water

You must be sure to provide your parakeet with fresh drinking water on a daily basis. You can give your bird water from the kitchen tap, but it should not be too cold. If you prefer, you can give your pet parakeet noncarbonated mineral water from time to time as a special treat. Mineral water is also healthy for your bird because it provides it with many beneficial minerals. You can usually find these listed on the label of the bottle. If your bird becomes ill, you should boil its water, allowing it to cool before giving it to your bird. It is okay to give a sick bird weakened black or chamomile tea, but only if recommended by your veterinarian.

Vegetables and Fruit

If you want your parakeet to stay healthy and live long, keep its beautiful plumage, and not get obese, you should give it plenty of fruits and vegetables that are in season and as fresh as possible. The best way to incorporate fresh produce into the parakeet's diet is to follow your own menu plan and give the bird some of everything that is good for it.

Raw vegetables: Eggplant, endive, green peas, young dandelion greens, corn kernels, fresh corn (especially if it is at the "milky" stage), Swiss chard, carrots, unsprayed lettuce, sorrel, spinach, parsley, radish, red beets, alfalfa, celery, zucchini, curly kale, brussels sprouts, and sweet potato.

Fruit: Fresh pineapple, apple, apricot, banana, pear, blackberries, strawberries, elderberries, gooseberries, mulberries, fresh figs, dates, raspberries, cherries, kiwi-fruit, mango, tangerine, melon, orange, peach, grapes, currants, guava.

Things to avoid: All kinds of cabbage, raw and green potatoes, green beans, lettuce sprayed with pesticides, grapefruit, rhubarb, plums, lemons, and avocados.

Important: Feed nothing directly from the refrigerator; all food should be at room temperature and have been washed, rubbed or dabbed dry, and peeled.

How to Offer Vegetables and Fruit

Fruits and vegetables that are of solid consistency, like pineapple, apples, pears, carrots, and zucchini, should be cut into slices or sections thick enough to stick between the cage bars. Soft fruits are cut into small pieces, mixed with berries, peas, shredded leafy vegetables, and perhaps some grated vegetables, and offered in a shallow bowl.

Don't be discouraged if your bird doesn't immediately realize what delicacies it is being given. Perhaps it just barely touches the food with its bill. If its taste buds come into contact with the juice of a fruit, the bird may then be brave enough to take a bite. It often takes days or even weeks before a parakeet develops a liking for fresh food and starts looking forward to it as a treat.

A practical holder for spray millet, in which even smallish pieces can be offered.

These parakeets are sharing a snack.

Parakeets that are already used to fresh food sometimes love to just peck and nibble at it. They may bite pieces off a slice of carrot or a piece of apple and leave some of them. The impulse behind this behavior is the pleasure of taking things apart; but minute quantities of the fruit are absorbed and supply necessary vitamins even if most of it is not eaten. When you consider how

An adult blue male and an adult green female.

A young parakeet perches on a bowl of fresh vegetables.

little a parakeet weighs, you can appreciate that though its body's need for these substances is crucial, it is small compared to ours.

Minerals and Trace Elements

Like people, parakeets need these substances only in minute quantities. Seeds as well as fresh foods contain small amounts. The most important, calcium and phosphorus, are present in the

This adult parakeet maintains its health and beautiful plumage with a proper diet.

mineral block the bird uses to sharpen its beak on and in the bird sand. When buying a mineral block, always watch for a note on the package saying something like "Calcium block, containing all elements necessary for strengthening the skeleton and forming feathers." Make sure you always have a stone in reserve, for quite often a bird will suddenly go to work avidly on the block in the cage, reducing it to nothing within a few hours after not having touched it for weeks.

Tip: Sepia shells, or cuttlebone, are also used for sharpening the beak, but they should *not* be given to female parakeets about to breed because these birds sometimes develop egg binding after gnawing on sepia shells.

Herbs and Wild Plants

Fresh foods can include herbs and wild plants because these resemble the things parakeets eat in the wild.

Your kitchen and garden can supply basil, chervil, and parsley to supplement the bird's diet.

In meadows (unfertilized ones) or along the roadside (but not along roads with automobile traffic), you can gather wild plants when you are out walking. Collect half-ripe and ripe seeds from annual grasses and wild millet, the leaves and flowers of bush vetch, tufted vetch, and cow vetch, open seedheads of pansies, flowers and fruits of hawthorn, and leaves and stems of dandelions, chickweed, shepherd's purse, and watercress.

Rinse all herbs and wild plants with lukewarm water, shake dry, and attach bunches of them to the cage roof with a clothespin.

Tip: If you notice your parakeet trying to "bathe" in the moist greenery, quickly offer the bathhouse with water or a shallow dish with a lot of damp greens for a "dew bath" (see page 26).

Enriching the Diet

✔ Spray millet is the most important supplement and is loved best by the birds. A highly nutritious and unadulterated natural food, it is ideal for breeding pairs, nestlings, and young birds, as well as for sick and weak ones.

✔ However, healthy, fully grown birds should not get more than a piece about 2 inches (6 cm) long per day. If they are given more, they will feed almost exclusively on the millet and get too fat. Attach the spray millet to the cage with a clothespin.

When a parakeet cleans its belly feathers, it draws each one through its beak singly to smooth and oil it.

✔ Special seeds, sold in small packages and under names that suggest that they promote easy molting, facilitate learning to talk, and so on, are birdseed mixtures that no doubt are exceptionally high in vitamins and proteins (so far no scientific analysis has been provided) but that a bird receiving a good balanced diet probably doesn't need. I am certain that these special foods have no effect on the ability to talk. Learning to talk is something the bird itself has to accomplish, and you have to help it by patiently repeating the phrases to be mastered over and over again (see page 39).

✔ Hearts, rings, sticks, wheels, and other shapes covered with seeds are sold as parakeet treats. No one knows whether the birds like them because of the taste or simply because they like to gnaw on things. The seeds are glued to the shapes with sugar syrup and honey. Fresh branches are also very healthy and provide "work" for a parakeet's beak.

✔ On the other hand, giving vitamin supplements seems very sensible to me since it is impossible to check the vitamin content of birdseed—the bird's dietary mainstay—or of fruits and vegetables. Vitamins are crucial to health. The smaller the organism, the more sensitive it is to the lack of vitamins. That is why it is advisable to add vitamins to the bird's drinking water. You can find multivitamins for birds in the pet food department of the supermarket or at the pet store. Look for the expiration date. Vitamins that are too old are useless.

What You Can Prepare Yourself

✔ Hard-boiled egg yolk mixed with a little low-fat cottage cheese is a valuable protein supplement. About half a teaspoonful a week

Directions for Sprouting Seeds

✔ Cover ½ teaspoonful each of birdseed, whole oat, and whole wheat kernels with ¾ of an inch (2 cm) water and let them soak for 24 hours.

✔ Rinse the seeds off with lukewarm water, let them drain, then put them in a glass dish and let stand, lightly covered, in the open at room temperature for 48 hours.

✔ As soon as the sprouts emerge from the seeds, offer them to the bird. Rinse them very thoroughly with lukewarm water first and drain well. If you wait another 24 hours, the sprouts will be bigger.

is beneficial. Be sure to remove uneaten egg food after an hour or two.

✔ Freshly cracked grain, which you may use in your own breakfast cereal, can also be given to the bird. Soak about a quarter of a teaspoonful a day in a little lukewarm water for your bird.

✔ Feed your bird sprouted seeds daily for three to four weeks at the following times: in the middle of winter and again in early spring, during the molt, when the female broods, and at times when the bird is not getting much fresh food. This will prevent deficiencies from developing. You can sprout the birdseed you buy at the pet store or whole oat and wheat kernels sold for sprouting at health food stores. As soon as viable seeds start to absorb water, a chemical reaction is triggered that results in sprouting. In the process, the vitamins, minerals, and trace elements present in the seeds are released and increase, which enhances the nutritional value of soaked and, even more, of sprouted grains and seeds.

Very important: Don't cover the seeds airtight or they will form mold. Sprouts mold

quickly at room temperature so you should throw out any sprouts not consumed within two hours.

Eating from the Table

It is hard to resist the charm of a tame parakeet walking daintily from plate to plate helping itself to a little bit of this and that—but moving around on the table among hot dishes

Two content adult parakeets: a green male and a blue female.

with foods that may be highly spiced or contain other things that don't agree with a bird's digestion is dangerous. The bird can get scalded, burn its tongue, or choke on hot spices. If you decide to let your parakeet join you at the dinner table all the same, you have to watch it constantly and have some foods

A varied diet consists of birdseed, spray millet, fruit and vegetables, herbs, and fresh drinking water.

prepared especially for it, things like a bit of boiled, cooled potato, a little dry white bread, some mildly seasoned vegetable, or some fruit. If the bird is in its cage in the same room when people sit down for a meal, it, too, will begin to eat—from its own dish.

Important Points About Diet

Healthy for the Bird

✔ Fill a cup with birdseed once a day; remove empty hulls at least twice a day.

✔ Offer a piece of spray millet about 2 inches (6 cm) long every day.

✔ Give a bowl of mixed fresh fruits and vegetables twice a day if you can, and provide as much variety as possible.

✔ Supply a little bunch of fresh herbs or wild greens daily.

✔ At intervals of four to six weeks treat your parakeet to a period of sprouted seeds.

✔ Supply fresh drinking water every day, perhaps mixed with a vitamin supplement.

A water dispenser keeps the drinking water clean because hardly any dirt can get into the narrow drinking trough.

✔ Make sure the bird always has a mineral block in the cage for sharpening its beak.

Harmful for the Bird

✔ Cold food fed directly from the refrigerator.

✔ Rotting or moldy food, even if the bad spots have been removed. Bacteria and fungi continue to grow hidden deep inside the food.

✔ Salty and spiced food, and, of course, plain salt, spices, and sugar.

✔ Chocolate and other sweets.

✔ Cream, butter, cheese, and other fats and fatty foods.

✔ Alcoholic beverages and coffee.

Make sure that you avoid the following:

✔ Depriving the bird of food, hoping a hungry bird will "eat out of your hand." This is sheer cruelty to animals.

✔ Small automatic food dispensers. I know from my own experience that these devices stop working when they clog up with dust or empty husks. If the food flow stops entirely, a bird may die of hunger. If you want to use an automatic feeder, make sure the opening and the seed collector at the bottom are large enough, and check daily to make sure the food runs through smoothly.

Please keep in mind: Parakeets are members of the parrot family, but their bills are not as strong as those of their larger relatives. They are able to dehusk seeds with their beak and their small, thick tongue, and they can take bites of soft fruit. Harder fruit and root vegetables, like apples and carrots, have to be grated or given in slices lodged firmly enough between the cage bars for the birds to be able to bite off pieces. Parakeets cannot hold onto pieces of food with their feet while eating them the way larger parrots do, and the keeper should therefore do what he or she can to make eating easier. For instance, many parakeets are especially fond of the small seeds on strawberries, but they can only get at them if you hold the berry steady. They also like grapes but can only eat them if they are cut in half. Then, if you hold half a grape up to the bird, it may dip into the grape and drink the juice with obvious enjoyment.

Converting to Fresh Food

Some parakeets persistently refuse to try fruit, herbs, or vegetables you offer them. They may ignore these healthy additions to their diet for years, until their keeper is utterly discouraged and gives up trying. But sometimes a little ingenuity and the ability to look at the world from the bird's perspective can result in convincing a parakeet of the value of fresh food after all. Therefore, some friends of mine,

who had long tried in vain to give their parakeet fruit and vegetables, finally decided to let the bird join them at breakfast, when there was always plenty of fruit and some health-food bread with whole grains in it. At first, the bird only nibbled a little on some dry bread, but when it saw that all the members of its "flock" were eating fruit, its interest was aroused and it wanted to taste some too. It wasn't long before it got used to eating fruit cut small for it, and from then on it waited with eager anticipation for its breakfast.

I have heard similar stories about other parakeets. One bird would only eat fresh food if its mistress started to eat a piece of fruit it had first spurned.

You can also try cutting fruits and vegetables into interesting shapes. There is a variety of commercially available pellets that come in colored shapes, which you might want to purchase for your bird.

HEALTH CONCERNS

The Sick Parakeet

If you observe any of the following behaviors, it is probably a good indication that your parakeet is sick: the bird sits on its perch and appears indifferent; the tail droops; the plumage is puffed up; the bill is tucked into the back feathers; or the bird avoids contact.

It is common for healthy birds to sleep on one leg, but some sleep on two legs. However, if you see your parakeet with its eyes half open and resting on both its legs, it may be in need of veterinary care. Or, the bird may blankly stare off into space, refusing to eat but drinking more than usual. A parakeet that displays any of these conditions should be treated right away before it loses its strength and can no longer balance on its perch. It won't be long before you see your parakeet lying flat on the floor of its cage. Do not hesitate to take your bird to the veterinarian for help.

Note: A bird is not sick if it tries to feed its avian partner, its plastic companion, or its bell or mirror with regurgitated seeds, or if it sneezes or yawns occasionally.

Helping a Sick Bird

It is crucial that the bird room be kept warm and quiet. You should provide a sick parakeet with its own cage if possible. Consult with your avian veterinarian to make sure that it is okay

These two healthy yellow and green parakeets enjoy nibbling at each other.

to give your bird lukewarm chamomile tea. You might want to consider treatment with an infrared light (see page 58).

Veterinarian Visits

When you notice signs of illness in your pet parakeet and there is no visible improvement within one or two hours, you should take the bird to the veterinarian as soon as possible, either that day or the following day at the latest. If you notice any alarming signs (refer to the table on page 59) you must consult your veterinarian at once. Most veterinarian offices in larger cities can be reached in emergencies at night or on holidays. Make sure that you have the phone number readily available and be prepared for such emergency situations.

Talking with the Veterinarian

A stool analysis is usually done on the spot or the results are available the next day. If it yields no clear diagnosis, the veterinarian will give the bird shots or other medications based on what he or she thinks is wrong. Be sure to have everything explained to you clearly, especially if biopsies of the skin, mucous membranes, or other tissue are suggested. Discuss in detail whether further treatments make sense, what the chances of success are, how the treatment will affect the bird, and whether there are alternatives. Ask also what would happen if you decided to reject certain treatments.

When using an infrared lamp, cover half the cage with a cloth, so that the bird can get away from the lamp's rays if it gets too hot.

Medication

If you have to give your bird medication, conscientiously follow the veterinarian's recommendations about dosage, length of therapy, and method of administration. Medications in liquid or powdered form are sprinkled or dribbled over the birdseed or added to the drinking water (tablets are crushed). If you do add them to the drinking water, however, you have to make sure the bird doesn't have access to a dripping faucet or can satisfy its thirst by eating juicy fruits and vegetables. If your bird stops drinking because of the taste of the medication, you will have to use a different technique. If you have to make your bird swallow drops, enclose its body loosely in your hand, bend the head slightly backward, and drip the required number of drops next to the tongue.

Questions the Veterinarian Will Ask

✔ How old is the bird?
✔ When did it first look sick?
✔ What did you notice particularly?
✔ Has the bird been sick before?
✔ Who treated it then and what drugs and other treatments were used?
✔ What kind of birdseed is the parakeet eating? (Be sure to take along a sample.)
✔ What does it drink?
✔ What kinds of fruit and vegetables has it been eating?
✔ Could it have nibbled on something poisonous?
✔ What other animals live in your household?

Infrared Light Treatment

If your bird requires this treatment, set up an infrared bulb of 150 to 250 watts 16 inches (40 cm) away from the cage in such a way that only half of the cage is exposed to its rays. This allows the bird to get out of the heated area if

A healthy parakeet produces droppings every 12 to 15 minutes. The drawing shows what these droppings should look like: There should be a dark rim around the white uric acid. Runny droppings can be a sign of illness.

Health Problems at a Glance

These signs may indicate only a passing indisposition.	*If accompanied by these symptoms, there is cause for alarm, and treatment by the veterinarian is required.*
Displaying apathetic behavior; avoiding contact.	Staggering; trembling; falling from perch. Possible infection?
Refusing to eat.	Cramping; partial paralysis. Vitamin deficiency? Tumor?
Breathing difficulties; frequent yawning (might be from lack of exercise/obesity).	Squeaking and whistling sounds when breathing; bird hangs from cage bar by the beak to breathe easier through stretched trachea. Pneumonia? Thyroid problems?
Frequent sneezing.	Sneezing with runny nasal secretion. Bad cold? Beginning of some other illness?
Mushy to runny droppings for over one or two hours.	Droppings are foamy, bloody, or strongly discolored; diarrhea persists. Alarm! Accompanying symptoms of many diseases (kidneys)?
Bird is unable to pass droppings.	Visible straining; cries of pain. Egg binding in females. Intestinal blockage?
Limping or dragging one leg or wing; light contusion caused by collision; lumps under the skin.	Leg or wing hangs down limply; no weight is put on one leg. Fracture? Fat deposits, thickening of the preen gland? Tumor? Other growth?
Bleeding from the cloaca or from wounds.	Internal bleeding. Injured blood vessel?
Restless nibbling on the plumage; continual frantic scratching.	Weight loss; dull plumage; feather plucking. Mites or other parasites? Emotional distress?
Spongy brownish growths on bill, cere, and feet.	Tiny mites that spread to other birds. Parakeet mange?
Many feathers fall out; normal molt (see page 63).	Constant molting; bare spots. Mites? Improper diet or hormonal imbalance?
Upper mandible overgrown; toenails too long.	Interferes with eating; toes catch in things. Beak or nails have to be trimmed.

A green parakeet preens its breast feathers.

A white-winged parakeet.

Even if your parakeet hasn't shown any signs of illness, make sure you know of a veterinarian who has experience treating pet birds.

it wants to (see drawing, page 58). Make sure there is enough drinking water available and place a bowl with steaming water near the cage to provide humidity. If necessary, leave the heat lamp on for two days, and turn it on again after a rest of one day. If the patient's health has visibly improved, move the heat lamp further away from the cage bit by bit so that the temperature drops very gradually.

Make sure, after you turn the infrared lamp off, that the temperature in the room stays even and that there are no drafts.

Important: In cases of partial paralysis—as when the bird is dragging one foot or one wing is drooping—or of cramping, the use of a heat lamp tends to be more harmful than beneficial. In such a case, consult an avian veterinarian as quickly as possible.

Diseases and Health Problems

Psittacosis

This disease is difficult to diagnose because it shows no clear-cut symptoms. Birds that have come down with psittacosis are apathetic, pass droppings that are too soft and often contain traces of blood, have the snuffles, and are short of breath, or the disease may manifest itself in conjunctivitis and slimy secretions at the lower eyelids. All these symptoms can occur singly or in combination. Because of this it is important to watch the bird carefully, treat it with infrared light when any of these ailments occur, and take the bird to the veterinarian if they persist.

In the past, psittacosis was greatly feared because humans, too, can be infected with it and because it was sometimes fatal. Imported parrots had to be quarantined because people thought the disease occurred only in these birds. Today we know that native songbirds as well as domestic poultry can get psittacosis, and the disease now usually goes by the name of ornithosis (*ornitho* as in "ornithology") rather than psittacosis (*psittakos* = Greek for "parrot"). In the meantime, drugs have been developed that effectively cure the disease in birds as well as in humans if it is treated in good time. If there are any questionable symptoms, the veterinarian can order a laboratory analysis of a fecal sample that will establish whether it is a case of ornithosis or not. Any occurrence of ornithosis has to be reported. Your veterinarian will tell you what has to be done in such a case.

If you or another family member should develop a severe respiratory disease, tell your doctor that you keep a budgie.

Misshapen Feathers

Feather malformations sometimes occur in older birds. Flight feathers, tail feathers, and contour feathers remain stuck in their sheaths with only a small brushlike tuft flaring out at the top. Sometimes feathers taper halfway up and then twist around their own axis. Nutritional deficiencies, hormone imbalances, poor blood supply, or cysts in the feather follicle can cause abnormal feathers, which should be treated by the veterinarian.

Feather Plucking

This unfortunate habit is not widespread among parakeets; it is usually the larger parrots that succumb to it. Still, feather plucking does occur in parakeets. The affected birds keep plucking feathers until bald and bloody

This sick parakeet is squatting apathetically on its perch with half-shut eyes, ruffled feathers, a drooping tail, and in an almost horizontal position.

spots appear. Many ornithologists ascribe this compulsive behavior to psychological causes, while others think that the birds accidentally discover the fluid inside the quills when preening and become addicted to it. Whatever the explanation, there is unfortunately no effective way to break a bird of this habit. The situation is most promising if the bird started plucking its plumage in reaction to a psychologically stressful situation, as when the usual caretaker has been away but can now again devote plenty of time to the bird. Usually, however, the cause is not this simple, especially in parakeets, in whom feather plucking is almost always a sign of some health problem. In these birds, feather plucking is usually associated with nutritional deficiencies, abnormal metabolism, or parasites. A parakeet that plucks its feathers should be taken to an avian veterinarian with experience in this area.

This drawing shows how the toenails should be cut. The blood vessels, which show faintly through the nail, must not be injured.

The Molt

The molt is not a disease, but for somewhat older parakeets it is a period of increased physical strain on the organism, during which the birds should get especially nutritious food and be kept evenly warm in a quiet environment. During the molt, birds replace their plumage. Many feathers are lost and replaced with new ones within a few days or weeks. During this time, the birds peck and nibble on their plumage more than usual and in a way that is clearly different from the typical preening. If the molt is particularly abrupt, the bird may temporarily be unable to fly and will then need your help. I used to stretch hefty strings in strategic places during these times, so that the grounded bird could get from the floor to the cage and from the cage to the bird tree.

French Molt

In the French molt, which is a disorder that affects parakeets, the feathers never develop completely. Nestlings can develop French molt; they are then usually unable to fly but do become tame. Such birds should never be housed together with healthy, breeding birds because the latter can become infected and may produce young with French molt.

BREEDING AND OFFSPRING

Is It a True Pair?

If you want your birds to produce offspring, you first have to make sure you have a true pair—that is, a male and a female or hen.

Male: If the cere above the bill is blue, this is a sure sign the bird is a male. If your bird is a lutino, albino, fallow, or a recessive pied (birds with splotches of color, also called harlequins), the cere will be pink.

Female: All female parakeets have buff-colored to light brown ceres.

Compatibility

If your two birds touch bills and preen each other, you will sooner or later see them get ready to mate, but it takes a while, for love at first sight is rare with parakeets.

It's quite possible that your two parakeets will get along famously without developing any sexual interest in each other. This is not surprising since they never had a chance to really choose their mate, a process that, in wild parakeets, is a crucial step toward forming a lifelong pair bond. If your pair shows no interest in courtship, mating, and breeding, you can

Young parakeets are independent and soon live in the cage after leaving the nest box.

add another male. Perhaps this second male will stir the reproductive instinct in the female.

It would be a mistake to add a second female to the pair. Females compete for a single male and fight viciously if they cannot get out of each other's sight.

Courtship Displays

The male, which at first acts rather cautiously toward the female, visibly gains self-confidence. More and more often he moves right next to her and eagerly taps his bill against hers. She, in turn, hacks at him less and less frequently to keep him at a distance. On the contrary, she now begins to approach him in a slightly bent-over posture and lets him feed her. In his growing sexual excitement the male tries to step on the female's tail, to which she responds by whirling around instantly and protesting vociferously. She seems to understand his intent, however, as there is never any active show of aggression.

The male now tries to impress his mate. He pulls on the bell in the cage with all his might, making it swing madly around his head, circles around the room in rapid flight, approaches again to give her a gentle nudge with the bill, then runs up and down in front of her excitedly,

The posture of a female parakeet ready to mate is almost coquettish. For a few seconds she stands still with her head thrown back and the tail raised high.

nodding and bowing continually. He keeps talking the whole time and makes the feathers on his throat and forehead stand on end. His eyes take on their typical courtship look with the pupils contracting into tiny dots.

The female doesn't seem to be overly impressed by all his eager devotion, but at some point she will indicate her readiness to mate in a charming gesture: She raises her tail straight up and throws her head back; then she remains motionless in this graceful pose. The male, in apparent confusion, alternates between putting one foot on her back and touching bills with her until he has gathered the courage to mount her. Holding onto the neck feathers of the female, he folds one or both wings around her and presses his cloaca against her so that his semen can get to her oviduct.

Owners and Breeding

Most parakeet owners will be content to use the cere color method to determine the sex of their bird. Since the bird has to be several months old before this technique can be used,

you may want to ask the store or breeder from whom you purchase the bird to have it sexed by the "feather sexing" or DNA method if the sex of the bird is important to you.

Feather Sexing

DNA or feather sexing is safe, painless, and 100 percent accurate. A feather that has a blood supply (called a blood feather) is plucked and you or your veterinarian send it to a lab that does this type of sexing. A parakeet's sex is only significant to people who intend to breed their birds. Both sexes make fine pets and are equally talented at mimicry.

A Word about Perches

If you have a pair of birds and hope to breed them, make sure that the perches in the cage are fixed in position so that they hold steady when two birds share the same perch. Shaky perches can interfere with the birds getting into position for copulation. You should also see to it that the perches are of sufficient diameter for the male bird to grasp the perch with one foot while placing the other foot on the hen's back.

Territoriality

Some people would like to breed their parakeets but hold back from doing so because they have heard or read that when tame birds breed they lose interest in their human companions and even become vicious toward them. This is not completely accurate. Your parakeet pair will become defensive of their territory (especially the nest box) and may peck at you if you invade it. This is certainly normal and explainable behavior, and it is not wise for you to do too much investigating of the cage and nest area because you may frighten the parakeets and interfere with breeding. However, if your birds were originally tame pets, they will become so again after the breeding season is over. Observing breeding and the raising of offspring can be a wonderful learning experience for both children and adults, so don't let fear of losing your bird's friendship deter you from experiencing it.

(above) A one-week old parakeet in the nest box.

(left) This young green parakeet is old enough to enjoy a free-flight landing on the couch.

(opposite page, top) A blue female and a green male; note the male's blue cere.

(opposite page, bottom left) This parakeet needs a lifetime companion.

(opposite page, bottom right) These two birds share blue coloring and a long-time friendship.

HOW–TO: BREEDING

The Nest Box

The first thing that you should do for your birds is to place a nest box in the cage or in the bird tree. You can buy a nest box, the dimensions of which should be 10 by 6 by 6 inches (25 × 15 × 15 cm). The top of the box opens up to provide easy access for observing the nest and its inhabitants. The inside of the box contains a block with a hollow. Your birds enter the box through the hole, which is in the long side of the box. This entrance hole has a perch right below it. Some owners prefer to cut a hole in the back wall of the cage and mount the nest box on the outside.

Life Changes

Do not be alarmed if your birds seem initially bothered by the presence of the box and do not readily enter it. This is normal. Eventually the female bird will be the one to investigate and she will hesitatingly begin her approach and exploration. At first she will probably look in the entrance hole before she gets the courage to momentarily slip inside for a better look. Before long, she will begin her work inside the box, making the hollow in the block deep enough for her offspring. She will remain inside the box for longer periods each day. Although she will permit the male bird to bring her food, she will probably not allow him to enter the nest. The male parakeet will be persistent and will eventually make his way inside the box (a female in the wild would never allow the male entry into the nest, but this is not the case for domestic parakeets).

The First Egg

Approximately eight weeks after the male and female mate, the female will deposit the first egg. Around this time, you should watch for the following signs: the female might make herself appear sleek and slender, spread out her wings, and tremble; her droppings will get very runny and she will pass larger amounts than normal; and her cere (above the bill) will get lighter in color and will be a smoother texture.

If the nest box is not ready in time and the first egg drops to the floor, the female will have difficulty keeping her balance on the perch. She will bite at the air, shake, and fan out her wing feathers; however, she should recover within a few minutes. If there is *no* nest box, or if the female is immature, she will not pay anymore attention to the dropped egg and she may even destroy it.

Time to Breed

If the first egg is deposited inside the nest box, the female will sit on the egg immediately and will rarely leave the box. Every other day she will continue to lay an egg until there are three to five eggs (there will rarely be more than this amount of eggs). Hatching will then occur in the same order and at the same interval of time as the eggs were laid. Parakeet eggs weigh about 2 grams. This is exactly the same weight as a chick that has just hatched (see page 80 for more on hatching).

Once the birds have hatched, the female only leaves the box to defecate, which is about three or four times daily. She sticks her head out of the box's entrance hole to get food and she is fed solely by the male. The female is very cautious and carefully checks out any situation, giving darting glances at any unfamiliar sound. The male stays within close proximity, keeps guard, and provides the female with the reassurances of short calls and singing; however, she must always assure herself.

Important Points for Success

✔ It is important for the female to hear the male close to the nest box. Avoid disturbing activities and noise in the room where the box is located because such disturbances can be bothersome and cause the female to stop breeding.

✔ When the female sits on her newly deposited eggs, she is not as easily disturbed. At this time you can occasionally lift the nest box cover to check on things without any problem.

✔ After about ten days you can take advantage of the female's brief periods of absence to check the eggs properly. Hold each egg up to a light; fertilized eggs are bluish and slightly opaque. They look darker than infertile ones, which are light and translucent.

✔ Remove infertile eggs only if there are more than four eggs in the clutch; otherwise, too great a change in the amount of eggs could bother the female and she might stop breeding.

✔ You should provide the proper environment to ensure that the embryos develop correctly. An even temperature of 72°F (22°C) should be maintained, fresh air should be provided, and the humidity level should be kept at 60 per-

Although parakeets are able to mate at 3 to 4 months, it is better to wait until they reach 10 to 11 months before breeding

cent. If you need to adjust the humidity, use a humidifier if you have one; otherwise, place a big bowl of water (covered with wire mesh) in the room.

✔ If there are droppings on the eggs, don't try to wipe or wash them off because this could be harmful to the embryonic chicks. A waxlike layer on the shell protects the eggs against infections.

✔ Once the baby birds have hatched, you should check the nest daily. A chick occasionally dies, and the decomposition of the body, which sets in quickly, would endanger the other nestlings.

UNDERSTANDING PARAKEETS

Over the years I have received several hundred letters from parakeet owners asking all kinds of questions. Many of the letters were from children who wanted to know the meaning of various striking ways of moving, repeated patterns of behavior, calls, or other habits of their bird. In most cases I had to answer that no two parakeets are exactly alike and that each bird has its own peculiarities, but there are some types of behavior that are common to all parakeets, such as the melodic whistling or the quiet whetting of the bill that is observed in a relaxed and happy parakeet. Not every sequence of movements is necessarily associated with a specific mood; rather, moods tend to be expressed through certain motions and calls common to the species.

Typical Movements

Stretching of the legs: Occasionally, a parakeet will stretch one leg and at the same time extend the wing of the same side. This gesture is comparable to the stretching we do when we get tired of sitting or standing in the same position. When the leg is pulled up again, the toes are often curled into a fist. If you notice that your parakeet is always stretching the same leg, or isn't executing the gesture at all,

Parakeets enjoy having their head scratched by a friend.

this might be the first sign of some abnormal weakness. Watch the bird carefully, and take it to the veterinarian, if necessary.

Resting on one leg: The stretching of the leg often ends with the leg being retracted into the ventral feathers. Of course, the pulling up of the leg is not always preceded by stretching. Parakeets also usually have one leg tucked close to the body in their sleeping stance, although many parakeets sleep standing on both legs. You have to know your bird and its habits well to be able to tell if such small deviations from the norm are just peculiarities typical of your bird or an indication that something isn't quite right. One thing you can safely assume is that if your bird is resting on one leg, it feels relaxed and is well.

Bill tucked into the back feathers: Parakeets are very limber and can turn their heads 180 degrees. They do this whenever they bury their bill in their slightly ruffled shoulder feathers. Most parakeets sleep in this posture, though they also assume it during the day in periods of inactivity. Sometimes they chirp very softly at the same time.

Raising the wings: Perhaps more often than they stretch their legs, parakeets raise their folded wings. This, too, is a relaxing kind of stretching, but birds also assume this posture when they are getting a little overheated; it allows them to give off some body heat. Often, however, raising the wings is simply a gesture of contentment or relief.

Extending the wings sideways: The wings are spread sideways if a bird wants to impress its mate or a rival. However, if it flattens its plumage, making itself appear extremely sleek and slim and, in addition, bites at the empty air, this may be a sign of extreme pain or fear.

Typical Activities

Preening the head: A parakeet cannot groom its head with its bill. If there is no companion to perform this labor of love, the parakeet has to resort to its toes for scratching and cleaning the head. To do this, it cannot raise its foot directly to the head, passing it in front of the wing, but instead sticks it around in back of the wing, which looks awkward and comical. Ornithologists regard the way birds raise their legs—either in front of or behind the wing—with considerable interest because the particular method used gives some clues about the evolutionary relationship between different kinds of birds.

A parakeet also grooms its head by rubbing it against the cage bars or a perch.

Flapping the wings: Young birds, in particular, flap their wings vigorously while holding

on tight to the perch on which they are sitting. This is a way of exercising the wing muscles, which still need strengthening. Adult parakeets also flap their wings if they haven't had a chance to fly for some time. Another time for wing flapping is at the end of the molt, when the loss of too many feathers all at once may have rendered the bird flightless and it cannot satisfy its urge for aerial exercise. Birds that flap their wings should be allowed to fly as soon as possible, unless you know for sure that they are unable to for some reason.

Yawning: All birds, including parakeets, yawn, opening their bills extremely wide. If your bird yawns all the time, you should air the room thoroughly. Being creatures of the air, birds are much more sensitive to stale air than humans are. By the way, yawning is just as contagious in birds as it is in people. If one begins to yawn, its partner or the whole flock in a flight will soon be yawning too. This contagiousness of mood is typical for parakeets. If one bird starts to preen itself, its neighbors will soon follow suit, and the same pattern dominates broodiness, sleeping, and eating.

Sneezing: Sometimes birds produce sounds that are very similar to our sneezing. However, avian sneezing is not caused by the same things as human sneezing; birds sneeze to clear their nasal passages.

Shaking the feathers: Parakeets always terminate a preening session with a good shake of the entire fluffed-up plumage. This makes sense, for the bill has dislodged minute dust

After laying an egg, a female parakeet retains her balance only with great effort. A sick bird suffering pain can look the same way.

After sleeping or sitting still for some time, a parakeet needs to stretch. It does this by extending one leg, along with the wing of the same side, backward.

particles that are sent flying to the floor by the shaking. Sometimes you will see a similar shaking motion when the bird hasn't been grooming itself at all. Birds almost always shake themselves before they engage in a new activity. If your parakeet has been resting, for instance, and decides to go and have a drink, it usually shakes itself first. Shaking also relieves tension. If a parakeet has been uneasy or alarmed for some reason, it will shake itself as soon as the tension lets up.

Whetting the bill: After every meal, and sometimes in between meals as well, a parakeet rubs its bill against its perch. In part this practice serves to clean the bill and keep the mandibles in good shape. That is why it is important that natural branches be available to be used this way.

Consciousness of the tail: Their tails seem to be particularly important to parakeets. The tail is cleaned, oiled, and smoothed more often than any other part of the body, and this grooming chore is never entrusted to a partner. Apparently, parakeets have a special sensory capacity that tells them whether their tail is being touched by some object, which is accepted as unavoidable, or by a living creature, which must be fought at all cost. It is an important point for anyone trying to win the bird's trust and not lose it. If you have a pair of birds, you will also see that the tail plays a role in the courtship display. When the male approaches the female with the intention of mating, he trips along the floor, trying repeat-

edly to step on her tail. She resists by dodging him cleverly but doesn't respond aggressively.

Alarm calls and shrieking: It is well known that parakeets sometimes shriek for prolonged periods. Up to now there has been no plausible explanation for these agitated vocalizations, which wild parakeets apparently don't produce, since no one has mentioned observing this behavior. I myself have owned parakeets for over 12 years but have never heard them shrieking. I have, however, heard them emit shrill alarm calls quite often, combined with abrupt departure from the branch they were

If a parakeet wants to scratch its head, it raises a foot up behind the wing.

perching on, even when there was no sign of a threat outside the window. This shows that parakeets, even when they have been bred in captivity for many generations, have not "forgotten" their original natural behavior.

Typical Capabilities

Vision: Like all birds that are active during the day, parakeets see the world in colors. This is to be expected since the colorful plumage of many birds serves definite functions in their social interaction. Birds also have almost panoramic vision because their eyes are located on the sides of the head, enabling them to spot enemies over a wide range and take cover. The area taken in simultaneously by both eyes is smaller than in humans, but parakeets can absorb 150 images per second. By comparison,

This parakeet is enjoying a nap, resting on one leg.

the human eye absorbs only 16. For fast-flying birds, quick detection of details is crucial to survival.

Hearing: It is not surprising that birds have an acute sense of hearing when you consider that they have to be able to communicate over large distances with calls and songs. Their hearing also has to be highly differentiated—that is, the birds have to be able to distinguish small differences in sound frequencies to be able to interpret all the different vocal expressions and respond appropriately. What sounds like uniform shrieking to the human ear is recognizable to a parakeet as a specific sequence of notes. This sequence of notes is recognized by a partner and can even be repeated "verbatim."

Affectionate nibbling is a common activity and often leads to a lifelong bond.

Taste: No studies have been done on the gustatory capacities of parakeets, but anyone who has watched one of these birds sample food at the family table knows that it goes after some things eagerly and pays no attention to others. I am convinced that parakeets have nerve endings that are highly sensitive to taste.

Smell: I myself have very little sense of how well parakeets can smell, but a parakeet expert I know is convinced that parakeets can smell just as well as we can.

Touch: There is no question that birds surpass humans in this area. Their tactile capacities are highly developed, as shown, for instance, by the fact that a breeding parakeet female is able to sense the chick's movements within the shell with her breed patch (a small, almost bare area on the breast with good blood circulation) and thus know when the chick is about to hatch. Birds also have a special sensitivity to vibrations, which makes them detect the slightest tremors. They even interpret the sources of such tremors correctly and thus have early warning of approaching enemies and natural events. Because of this sensitivity to vibration, the cage of a parakeet should be in a place that is absolutely stable.

Tip: The vibration of the refrigerator motor can frighten a parakeet. Never put the cage near the refrigerator, even for a moment.

Embarrassment: A parakeet that is all set to fly spontaneously up to a trusted human may, if at the last moment it notices something new and visually striking in the person, stop, bewildered, and begin to preen itself instead of taking to the air. This is a bird's way of expressing embarrassment. My parakeet Manky used to enjoy playing with marbles on my desk. He would run after them or toward them, ready to give them a kick. But if two marbles rolled toward him simultaneously from the side instead of from straight ahead, this seemed somehow ominous to him, and he would immediately run to his food dish and start eating.

The Nature of Their Skills

When you read in the next few pages how parakeets live and survive in their Australian homeland, you will gain a better understanding of why nature has equipped these birds with so many skills and abilities.

General Description

Parakeets are part of the Psittacinae, the seventh subfamily of the parrot family. They are the only species of their genus, which is included in the tribe Platycercini (rosellas and allies), and there are no subspecies.

Scientific name: *Melopsittacus undulatus.* The first part of this Latin name comes from the Greek and means "singing parrot." "Undulatus" comes from the Latin word "unda," wave, and refers to the birds' undulating markings. In English, the birds are also known as "budgies," short for budgerigar, or as shell parakeets.

Origin: Australia

Habitat: Shrubby grasslands in Central Australia, especially along shallow streams with intermittent water flow (called "creeks" in Australia).

Original wild form: Green with a yellow mask and wavy black and yellow markings on the back of the head, the upper back, and the wings.

Overall length without tail: 6¼ to 7 inches (16–18 cm)

Tail: 3 to 3½ inches (8–9 cm)
Weight: 1 to 1.4 ounces (30–40 g)
Life expectancy: 12 to 14 years
Sexual maturity: At three to four months of age
Size of clutch: Three to five eggs
Egg laying: At intervals of two days
Beginning of incubation: After the first egg
Length of incubation: 18 days
Nestling period: 28 to 32 days

Nomadic Life

Living conditions in the hot, arid climate of central Australia are extremely harsh; sometimes it doesn't rain for months or even years at a time. The temperature in the morning and evening is 100°F (38°C) and climbs to 113°F (45°C) and higher during the day. Parakeets, therefore, spend the midday hours sitting in groups of 50 or so high up in the eucalyptus trees that grow along the creeks. They stay in the trees quietly and unobtrusively and, with their cryptic coloring, are practically invisible. This quiet way of life during the dry season is also due in part to the need to conserve water. The less active a creature is, the less water it uses up. The parakeets forage on the ground for food early in the morning and toward evening. At night the temperature drops very rapidly; after midnight it can go below freezing. These cool and sometimes downright cold nights luckily produce dew that the birds rub off the grass in the morning and that they fall back on for drinking water during dry periods. However, if there is water in the streams or in rock declivities,

When in a fighting mood, male parakeets threaten each other with open beaks and use their feet to kick the opponent in the chest.

parakeets drink about every three hours. Some other parrots drink only in the morning and evening. If there is no rain for long periods, the grasses and other plants dry up, and the few seeds are soon all eaten; then the parakeets are forced by the scarcity of food to set off in search of new pastures.

Misconceptions

One misconception about the needs of parakeets is demonstrated by owners and breeders who keep their birds in outdoor aviaries all year round without providing a heated shelter. These people argue that parakeets are used to severe weather since they survive cold nights in their native areas. It is true that parakeets do survive below-freezing weather in our temperate zones, but Mr. H. J. Michaelis, who knows a great deal about parakeets, has expressed the situation aptly: Parakeets do survive cold winters in outdoor aviaries, but they aren't really living; they merely vegetate. After all, in Australia the temperature drops below freezing for only a few hours at a time during the night, and not for weeks on end.

The parakeet's modest need for water gives rise to another misunderstanding. Under normal circumstances parakeets drink more frequently than other members of the parrot family do, but they drink much less at a time. Experiments have shown that parakeets can survive without water for up to 28 days at a temperature of 86°F (30°C) and a humidity of only 30 percent. Dr. Karl Immelmann comments: "In spite of the ability to do without water for considerable periods of time—which no doubt represents an adaptation to 'emergency' conditions—parakeets stay close to water if they can."

It is incorrect, therefore, to maintain that parakeets are perfectly comfortable in extended periods of below-freezing temperatures and that they don't need anything to drink.

What is correct is that parakeets are comfortable when it is warm. They become inactive only when it is very hot, and thanks to their plumage they can resist the cold of freezing weather for short periods. They are most alive and active in temperatures about 68°F (20°C). It is also true that parakeets like to take frequent small drinks of water and that they enjoy baths.

Breeding in the Wild

When, in the course of their wanderings, parakeets come to an area where it has recently rained or where rain is still falling, their whole way of life changes. Rain brings moisture and cooler weather. It makes plants grow green again, and there will soon be abundant supplies of half-ripe seeds, which are indispensable for raising baby parakeets. The males immediately start going through their courtship rituals to put the females into a broody mood, and the females get busy looking for suitable nesting cavities. Holes high up in eucalyptus trees are ideal. The female enlarges the inside of the cavity with her beak, makes sure there is a bowl-like hollow in the bottom, and works on the entrance hole. The fine chips produced by her beak-work serve as padding for the eggs and later for the nestlings.

Since small contingents of the large flying flock always stick together, groups of a few closely spaced trees become hives of avian activity. Several breeding pairs usually nest in the same tree. The courtship activity of the

male and the busy work of the female are contagious. Within a few days the tree holes are occupied, matings take place, and the first eggs are about to be laid in the protective cavities.

In nature, parakeets communicate with each other with certain calls, thus maintaining vocal contact with each other.

One rarely catches sight of a female; they brood the eggs steadily, emerging from their holes only to relieve themselves. While they sit on the eggs, the females are fed by the males. They get off the clutch only briefly and stick their heads out of the entry hole to receive food. In the wild, the male is not allowed into the nest cavity.

Incubation

The females lays an egg every other day, and incubation begins as soon as the first egg is laid. At regular intervals the eggs are turned and the ones on the outside are rolled to the center of the nest. After 18 days, when a chick is ready to hatch, it has already communicated that fact to its mother with soft peepings from inside the shell. It has also set to work on the inside of the shell with its "egg tooth," a thorn-shaped projection of the bill. It takes the chick 20 hours of chipping while rotating continually and pushing until it is free of its shell. Sometimes the mother helps by breaking off small bits of the shell.

The chicks hatch in the same order the eggs were laid. Naked and blind, they immediately disappear under the mother's plumage and are fed by her. When several chicks have hatched, the oldest one is always first in line for feeding

A pair of parakeets mating. The excitement makes the pupils contract so that they show up only as black dots in the middle of the white iris.

and receives food from the mother's crop while the youngest initially gets predigested food from the mother's glandular stomach (proventriculus).

Life in a Flock

After the young leave the nesting cavity, the father still looks after them for about two weeks. After that they are fully independent and live together with the juvenile birds of the entire flock, while the parents, if there is sufficient food supply, are busy with their next brood.

First Attempts at Courtship

Even before the young birds, which have only recently left their parents, undergo their first molt they begin to engage in courtship displays. At first it is only the males; they woo not only females their own age, but also, and preferably, ones that are already busy working

Pair bonds between parakeets last for life, until one of the partners dies.

on a nesting cavity. In contrast, young females tend to favor older males.

If a female doesn't like the courting male, she makes aggressive hacking motions toward him when he approaches, but if he meets her fancy, she bills and coos with him and soon lets him feed her and scratch her head.

Marriage for Life

Once a bond has been formed between a pair of parakeets, it usually lasts for life, as it does in most parrot species. This makes especially good sense for parakeets because then the birds don't have to waste time choosing mates. When a flock finds itself in an area where conditions for breeding are good, even the youngest members can settle down to the breeding business without first having to find partners. They are already paired and can go about their mating displays, the search for nest sites, and reproduction without delay.

Molting in a Hurry

The only time parakeets are sure to stay in the same place for a while is when they breed. That is why they also use this time to partially replace their plumage in a so-called "soft molt"; then, when they have to set out on long journeys again, their plumage is intact and ready.

Enemies

Parakeets are always aware of what is going on above them because originally, attack from higher-flying raptors was their main threat. They don't have an innate warning system ori-ented to enemies on the ground and are therefore easy prey to cats that have been introduced into Australia. Other birds competing for nesting cavities represent another danger. Although female parakeets defend their cavities and their eggs or young with great courage against intruders, they don't always prevail.

Communicating with Each Other

Parakeets are considered the quietest of the Australian parrots. Their vocal repertoire is less varied than that of many of our native songbirds. We have already mentioned that during the dry season parakeets keep so quiet that many observers become aware of their presence only by accident. During the resting periods their cryptic green coloring lets them completely fade into the foliage of the eucalyptus trees on which they perch. Since they feel safest when high up in the air, they congregate near the tops of the trees. From there, their soft twitterings hardly reach the ears of bird-watchers. When the birds forage on the ground, they usually remain quiet, too; only occasionally is a louder call heard. This call, which serves to maintain contact within the flock, always sounds the same to our human ears, but parakeets not only understand the message of the call, "We are here, where are you?" but can also tell by fine nuances of sound which individual bird it comes from.

Nuances of communication are even more important when the active reproductive phase of life starts. Now it is a matter of maintaining a minimum distance between birds so that the communal life of the flock can go on without the interference of aggressive acts, while at the same time respecting the privacy of the individual pairs.

Development of the Young

1st to 5th day: The chick's eyes are still shut and it is fed while lying on its back.

6th day: The eyes begin to open.

7th day: The primaries start to grow in.

8th day: The chick can hold up its head and take its first steps.

9th day: The tail feathers begin to grow in.

12th day: All the down feathers have grown in.

17th day: The young reaches the adult weight of 1 ounce (30 g).

28th day: The flight and tail feathers have almost reached their full length. The young bird can fly and leaves the nest.

38th day: The plumage is fully formed, but the coloration is somewhat duller than that of the parents.

3rd to 4th month: Prenuptial molt. The new plumage is similar to that of adult parakeets, and the birds are sexually mature.

INFORMATION

Books

Piers, Helen. *How to Take Care of Your Parakeet.* Hauppauge, NY: Barron's Educational Series, Inc., 1993.

Radford, Elaine. *Parakeets Today.* Neptune, NJ: TFH Publications, 1996.

Vriends, Matthew M. *The New Bird Handbook.* Hauppauge, NY: Barron's Educational Series, Inc., 1989.

Wolter, Annette and Monika Wegler. *The Complete Book of Parakeet Care.* Hauppauge, NY: Barron's Educational Series, Inc., 1994.

Magazines

Bird Talk
P.O. Box 6050
Mission Viejo, CA 92690

The AFA Watchbird
P.O. Box 56218
Phoenix, AZ 85079-6218

Cage & Aviary Birds
Prospect House,
9-15 Ewell Road
Cheam, Sutton, Surrey, SM3 8B2
England

Organizations

American Budgerigar Society
1704 Kangroo
Killeen, TX 76541

The Association of Avian Veterinarians
P.O. Box 811720
Boca Raton, FL 33481-1720

Aviculture Society of America
P.O. Box 5516
Riverside, CA 92517

The Avicultural Society of Queensland
c/o Mr. Ray Garwood
19 Fahey's Road
Albany Creek, 4035, Queensland
Australia

Bird Clubs of America
P.O. Box 2005
Yorktown, VA 23692

The Budgerigar Society
57, Stephyn's Chambers,
Bank Cour
Marlowes, Hemel Hempstead, Herts
England

The Golden Triangle Parrot Club
P.O. Box 1574, Station C
Kitchener, Ontario N2G 4P2
Canada

Photo Credits

 Joan Balzarini: pages 8 (bottom), 9 (top right, bottom left), 12, 16 (bottom left), 40, 41, 48 (top), 64, 68 (top), 69 (bottom right), 81; Matthew M. Vriends: pages 8 (top), 69 (bottom left), 80 (bottom); B. Everett Webb: front cover, inside front cover, back cover, inside back cover, pages 2–3, 4, 9 (top left), 16 (top, bottom right), 17, 20, 24, 25, 28, 32, 33, 37, 44, 48 (bottom), 49, 52, 53, 56, 60, 61, 68 (bottom), 69 (top), 72, 76, 77, 80 (top), 85.

Important Note

 People who are allergic to feathers or feather dust should not keep birds. If you think you might have such an allergy, consult your doctor before acquiring a bird. Psittacosis is at this point quite rare in parakeets (see page 62), but the disease can give rise to life-threatening conditions in both humans and parakeets. That is why you should take your parakeet to the veterinarian if you suspect it might have contracted the disease and visit your own doctor if you have cold or flu symptoms. Be sure to tell the doctor that you have birds.

English translation © Copyright 1999, 1990 by Barron's Educational Series, Inc.

© Copyright 1989 by Gräfe and Unzer GmbH, Munich, Germany.
The title of the German book is *Wellensittiche*

Translated from the German by Rita and Robert Kimber
Consulting Editors: Matthew M. Vriends, Ph.D. and Arthur Freud

All inquiries should be addressed to:
Barron's Educational Series, Inc.
250 Wireless Boulevard
Hauppauge, NY 11788
http://www.barronseduc.com

Library of Congress Catalog Card No. 99-15227

International Standard Book No. 0-7641-1032-2

Library of Congress Cataloging-in-Publication Data
Wolter, Annette.
 [Wellensittiche. English]
 Parakeets : a complete pet owner's manual : everything about purchase, care, nutrition, breeding, and behavior / Annette Wolter ; drawings by Karin Heckel ; [translated from German by Rita and Robert Kimber].
  p. cm.
 Originally published: New York : Barron's Educational Series, c1990.
 Includes bibliographical references (p.).
 ISBN 0-7641-1032-2 (pbk.)
 1. Budgerigar. I. Title.
[SF473.B8W6413 1999]
636.6'864—dc21   99-15227
                CIP

Printed in Hong Kong

9 8 7 6 5 4 3 2

Some parakeets become so tame and friendly that they like to perch on their owner's shoulder for hours. You can learn how to hand-tame your pet parakeet, and before long, a beautiful bird such as this could be sitting on your shoulder, chatting in your ear.